How to Sell to Men

Without Wearing a Low-Cut Dress

Deborah Gardner

BRYAN,
PERFORM YOUR BEST!
DEBORAH

Published by Deborah Gardner.

Design and layout by Mullins Creative, Inc.
www.mullinscreative.com

ISBN 978-0-9821440-0-8
Printed and bound in the United States of America

www.DeborahGardner.com

Dedication

To all the women who want to make a difference
by becoming successful and profitable in what has been considered
a man's world, and …

To all the men who unselfishly contributed their beliefs,
stories, and experiences in order for women to better understand
them. This truth will allow both genders to conduct business
transactions so everyone wins.

Testimonials

"Just showing up creates sexual tension ... ladies, be smart in business ... this book will guide you to generate greater income in a very respectful way."

~ Shanna McCoy, Vice President Sales & Marketing,
Conference Services International

"There is no doubt, Deborah is an exceptional sales professional who will keep you from bringing just one dimension to the negotiating table. Just remember what you're after—the SALE!"

~ Bruce MacMillan, President & CEO,
Meeting Professionals International

"Reputation is about earning credibility, not expecting it. You must build credibility so others are confident about doing business with you. One way to earn credibility ... read this book ... a must for anyone interested in selling and buying in a respectful, honest manner."

~ Michele C. Wierzgac, Speaker & Author,
The Forward Thinker™, Michele & Company®

"Practical, fun and pertinent! A terrific, easy read that bares it all. Enjoy, and see a great return on investment. Having worked directly with Deborah and seeing her succeed in sales, this book unveils many of her secrets."

~ Brad Walker, Vice President & General Manager,
The Brown Hotel

Acknowledgements

I would like to acknowledge the following family members, friends, and business partners:

- ~ My wonderful husband, Jerry, for loving me for who I am—thank god! Honey, you bring out the best in me.

- ~ My parents, Joseph and Ruth Ann Gardner, for their 50-plus years of marriage, proving to me that love conquers all.

- ~ Mark Mikelat, my excellent book coach and unbelievably patient person, who handled my millions of questions throughout every writing session. He helped me learn to write better!

- ~ My wonderful and talented father, Joedy Gardner for drawing the chapter illustrations.

- ~ Brandi Hollister and Vickie Mullins of Mullins Creative for the interior layout, book production and cover design assistance; Barbara McNichol, my incredible editor; and Ranee A. Spina for the cover concept and layout. Working with these experienced and talented women inspired me. They reinforced that the information in this book is the best thing I can share with all women. Women power!

- ~ My fabulous friends around the world, who encouraged and supported me throughout the educational process of writing this book. I wish I could name you all, but that would be a book in itself. Thank you for believing in me.

The special group of successful friends and business partners who had faith in the idea of this book. Their incredible talents and skills provided significant contributions. This indispensable task force includes Bill Morton, Christina Tzavellas, Phil Lavigne, Karolyn Kiburz, Jan Aksztulewicz, Danette Mitchell, Tom Caprino, Rachel Bohl, Valerie Linder, Michele Wierzgac, Steve Tyra, Connie Gutierrez, and Jacqueline Vuckovic. It was an amazing process—from gathering everyone's information and stories on a flipchart to celebrating the completion of this great book. My sincere gratitude goes to these fine and caring individuals.

Table of Contents

Foreword

When I first heard Deborah tell me about How to Sell to Men Without Wearing a Low-Cut Dress, *I was against it!*

But the more I thought about it, I was still against it!

Then I wondered, "How would I want my daughter, sister, or wife to dress in the world of sales?" That's when that giant light bulb over my head nearly burned a hole in my hat—a BFO (blinding flash of the obvious).

If women want to be truly professional in sales, they MUST be valued for their skills and knowledge, NOT their cleavage. I can't believe I said that! What an incredible admission for a knuckle-dragging Neanderthal like me!

This book goes far beyond my rants and twisted reality to give you important, specific ways to trade in cleavage for professionalism when selling to men (sexual innuendo implied but not required). You will learn a lot from its true stories and examples that will enhance both your self esteem and your bank account. Ignore its advice at your peril; apply it and you'll get great sales results!

~ Steve Tyra, Humorist

Introduction

Why do women feel they need to wear a low-cut dress to get what they want?

Women around the world get up every day, walk into their closets, and ask themselves, "Should I wear a low-cut dress or should I not?" It's an on-going question, whether a woman is heading to the office, a party, a sporting event, dinner with friends—or to a sales appointment with a man.

How to Sell to Men Without Wearing a Low-Cut Dress reveals how many saleswomen worldwide use such ploys to seek attention from male customers or clients and get what they want in business transactions—whether it be to obtain a signed contract, the best deal on a new car, or a promotion. Wearing seductive or revealing clothing is a worn-out strategy women have used for centuries to draw attention to them while closing a sale with men. The "low-cut dress" is an analogy that covers all manner of suggestive behaviors, such as displaying a leg or a navel or allowing locks of hair to fall in the face. It can apply to how women talk or how they sway their hips when they walk.

Well, listen up, ladies! Behavior speaks much louder than words, and it dictates your success—or ultimate failure. Self-defeating "low-cut dress" behavior continues to negatively affect women's abilities to advance in business by distracting from or taking the place of using their intelligence and skills. So, protect your heart, zip it up—the low-cut dress, that is!

This book helps women understand these behaviors and eliminate the perception that such actions will cause any real advancement or gain them respect. Instead, it presents more suitable strategies for closing a sale with their most profitable customers—men! Success and advancement can be solidly achieved with skillful negotiating, presenting, and closing, along with the other simple strategies this book provides.

In the business world, women often play "nice" while men play "to win." Men have a focus, a competitive approach to getting the job done. Women want to impress others, thinking that's the way to win business. Some women go as far as conducting business in gentleman's clubs or bars just to get a contract signed. Sure, there is plenty of business conducted in a gentleman's clubs or bar atmosphere. However, are sales women really comfortable with this format or just doing what they can to close the deal?

It's the 21st century, folks! Why do women even believe they still have to use the same old denigrating strategies to close a deal—strategies that, in the long run, make it difficult to achieve their goals of professionalism and success? How can women sell their products and services with an everyday business approach as men do?

Perhaps saleswomen try these strategies on men because they haven't been used to selling to men and don't know how. They've been focused on selling to women—and rightly so in certain markets, as research shows that 80 percent of all household spending is controlled by women. But males still dominate both the earning and decision-making in the business world.

Wake up, saleswomen! Men are buyers too! We cannot afford to ignore this fact. Although men may make up a smaller percentage of all buyers, they spend top dollars on expensive items. This is a huge factor for saleswomen to consider when strategically selling and marketing to men.

Marketing companies are noticing that the buying sectors of the population (i.e., genders, generations) differ in consumer behaviors. This is especially true of men. Companies that sell satellite TV have determined men to be their most profitable customer. Thus, their media-buying strategies shifted to target the male consumer.

Consider the automobile industry, which takes great interest in the difference between men and women buyers. Just ask MSN Autos. Its studies show if you ask any woman if she wants to buy a sports car for which the starting manufacturer's suggested retail price is more than $80,000, she almost certainly wouldn't be seriously interested or able to afford it. The studies indicated that such a vehicle definitely attracted a higher proportion of men buyers and pitifully few women. Now, ask any man if he wants to spend his money to buy a four-cylinder car for around $18,000. In this case, a larger percentage of women were prospective buyers than men. What does this mean for saleswomen, especially those selling cars? If men are buying, it more often means *huge* sales, which result in *huge* profits and *huge* payoffs for saleswomen.

The point is that, like it or not, men still earn more than women and can buy high-ticket items. Therefore, selling to men results in bigger profits than selling to women. This book will help saleswomen make a major difference for themselves and propel their advancement in the business world. And it will show women how to take advantage of these opportunities *without* having to wear a low-cut dress.

———————

My interest in supporting women who sell to men has its roots from my childhood. I grew up with a military family's lifestyle, and I was taught differently than most "daddy's little girls." Specifically, I was taught to fight for what I believed in. Not the belief that I deserved to sit in the front row of the school bus or date the football quarterback, but to fight for ME!

As a collegiate competitive swimmer and then one of the first female sportscasters, I experienced what it takes to win as an individual and as a team player. After that, I was able to advance my career in the hospitality sales profession for 24 years. I consistently exceeded sales goals as high as $3.5 million annually while servicing many decision makers. In 2007, I parlayed those learning experiences into my own company, COMPETE BETTER NOW! With my passion for sales and working with a wide range of buyers, "the need to know and apply" transpired. I became fascinated with the buying behaviors, researching sales process differentials and strategic positioning between the two genders.

I began my research by observing and talking with saleswomen who had been struggling in their business dealings with men. This process expanded into interviewing hundreds of women around the world while gathering questions on how to sell to men. Some of the more frequently asked questions are—

- Is it possible for women to do business with men?

- Can women really communicate with men?

- How do women handle the "Good Old Boys" club?

- What's the payoff for women to know how to sell to men?

And even—

- How do women get hold of the remote control?

The next step was to address these questions to hundreds of *men* from around the world in many different industries and professions. I interviewed a total of 430 men who expressed their thoughts, opinions, and points of view. They offered examples, stories, and experiences from working with saleswomen. I believed this approach would help both genders understand what it takes to conduct business together.

The entire process has resulted in a winning combination. Saleswomen are learning how to successfully work with men; men are successfully doing business with saleswomen who can operate on a level playing field and use their skills to benefit everyone.

With both sets of interviews and observations in hand, members of my special task force gathered to contribute their own stories, facts, and experiences, which enhanced the research. Compiling and organizing this "gender to gender" sales information resulted in this amazing book. Please note, this book is not an essential guide for all women, a manual on how to deal with men in general, a sales policy booklet, or even a dress code to follow. It's about discovering who you are as a saleswoman. What talents and abilities do you have to close the sales deal with your male customers?

In addition, it's about learning to approach any sales situation with the utmost confidence and positive mindset. With this approach, you can provide the best service and solutions *and* increase your sales profits. The new strategies culled from all the interviews will allow you to successfully sell to men, while leaving the low-cut dress in the closet.

Testosterone Quotations

The hundreds of men I interviewed came from around the world including Italy, India, Australia, United Kingdom, China, Singapore, Belgium, Germany, Norway, Nigeria, and the United States. In gathering their opinions, I saw how they supported the view that wearing a low-cut dress in business is not the best strategy for selling to men. Throughout the book, you'll see "testosterone quotes" for saleswomen that provide men's truthful perspective on how women can best sell to them. Here are three examples you'll find throughout this book:

"The more a woman's body is covered up, the more respect men tend to have toward them. Business protocol is to dress and conduct yourself professionally, which is what I expect from anyone I do business with."

~ Bill Morton, Sales Hospitality,
Phoenix, Arizona

"Any woman who uses the low-cut dress as a component for securing the sale must also understand that most men will believe consummating the sale includes a bonus offer."

~ Ross Shafer, Comedian,
Ross Shafer Productions,
Anaheim Hills, California

"Life lesson—when a woman exposes something ... she is really hiding something else!"

~ Roger Rickard Sr., VP Sales,
don anderson incorporated,
Sacramento, California

The Power of Lingerie

Chapter One
SEX Sells!

S usan, a highly intelligent woman, works for a prestigious hotel company in downtown Los Angeles. As a sales manager, she has handled accounts for the east coast territory for more than five years. She's tall and slim, good-looking fashionable woman who takes pride in her appearance and profession.

One day, Susan wore a tailored brown business suit with a knee-length skirt and a button-up red lingerie blouse with shoes to match. Her straight light brown hair brushed her shoulder when she moved. She excitedly strode into her office at the hotel to prepare for an important appointment. Susan had worked extremely hard for months to get this prospective client to book his annual meeting at her facility. If Susan closed this deal, she would be promoted to director of sales, which had been her career goal in the hospitality industry for a long time.

When the prospective client, an experienced business man, arrived, he suggested their conversation take place in the hotel lobby. He intently listened to Susan's presentation suggestions for making his company's annual meeting a success. The sales conversation moved along smoothly as Susan introduced this gentleman to staff members walking by. The general manager stopped to meet him and even the chef delivered some snacks. As the contract negotiation continued, Susan thought he seemed agreeable to her suggestions. Her mood soared.

Then at one point, Susan crossed her legs for a more comfortable sitting position, unintentionally revealing a butterfly tattoo on her ankle. Immediately the businessman noticed it. He leaned over and actually put his hand on her leg to touch the tattoo. The sales conversation came to a sudden halt.

"So, is that a real tattoo?" he queried.

"Well, yes," replied Susan, "but let's discuss the details to the contract clause at this time."

"I bet you're pretty wild outside office hours—right?" He wouldn't let up.

Susan tried to get him back on track. "I'd like to make sure your contract is satisfactory to you, so let's continue our negotiation process."

"I would be more satisfied," he replied, "if we could discuss the contract another time. I'm interested in knowing more about what made you decide to get this wild tattoo."

Exasperated, Susan excused herself from the table. While pacing the hallway, she nervously tried to figure out how she could escape the situation without being rude, or more important, without losing the contract. How could she salvage the meeting without embarrassment? She couldn't call her office and share what was going on with any co-worker. How would that look when she was aiming for a promotion? Susan felt stuck!

Five minutes later, she returned to the lobby, projecting a less-than-genuine smile. She sat down covering her tattoo as best as she could, and continued the conversation as if nothing had happened. The prospective client continued to look at her with an expression of interest that exceeded their business negotiations. Susan started to rush through the sales process. At the end, she asked him for his annual meeting business. He responded with, "Susan, next time if you want to sell the goods, you need to show some goods."

Then, to her immense surprise and relief, he picked up the pen and signed the contract.

⸻⬦⸻

Let's face it—SEX SELLS! For centuries, society has projected a distorted message that men are superior to women but are subservient to women's appearance from a sexual standpoint. We know this is still true today from surfing the Internet, observing billboards, reading magazines, and watching movies, television shows, and commercials. Sex is a powerful motivator. And when it comes to attracting men's attention, marketers know that men's brains fall below their belts when a beautiful woman is involved.

Remember the famous Go Daddy commercial played during several Super Bowl telecasts when a sexy model walks into the office, causing the workers to be distracted? The model had nothing to do with the message for Go Daddy other than to grab men's attention so they'll watch the commercial. But now, whenever they think of Go Daddy, their thoughts are inextricably (although perhaps subconsciously) linked to the sexy model. Their decision to use Go Daddy could easily be based on her presence in the commercial, not necessarily on the product itself.

If we removed "sex" from advertisements or conversations around everyday decision-making, the world would be a different place. True, it may be more boring or less tantalizing, but in reality, the world is sexually driven.

Nonetheless, do women have to face the challenge of being regarded as a sex object in everyday business? What was Susan's prospective client clearly stating? Was Susan giving the wrong impression that led him to believe he deserved more than the business contract? How can the gap of equality between men and women be closed if situations such as Susan's persist?

What about the other extreme, some women take advantage of sexual implications to land business. Rhonda, a pharmaceutical saleswoman, enjoys wearing seductive clothing to work. When she conducts sales presentations, her co-workers notice her wearing even shorter skirts. Her male clients and prospects undoubtedly enjoy her flirtatious manner and sexy attire. With this type of strategy, Rhonda gets the sale virtually every time, which makes the rest of the team look like slackers and just not as good at closing the sales.

Mark, a co-worker, tries to talk to Rhonda on occasion to let her know how co-workers are appalled by her appearance and behavior. From his perspective, he suggests that she at least leave something for the imagination. However, Rhonda says her attire works for her and claims the others are just jealous. Mark believes that Rhonda pays a price; she never gets to build professional relationships with her clients because they view her as a sex object. But in Rhonda's view, the sales process meets her needs.

Mark knows that Rhonda's clients don't really care that she's being unprofessional; they just love the attention she gives them. He even admits it's great to hang around her; it makes him feel "manly" that he works with such a beautiful woman. And at times, even Mark gets caught up in the spell she casts with her sexy attire. However, he remains uncomfortable with the unnecessary strategy of using her sex appeal to obtain business by saying, "The real issue is that Rhonda is the type of woman who would do whatever it takes to get the business. She swears like a sailor and has a rude attitude toward others. She would throw you under a bus the minute she had the opportunity. More people are starting to see this true side of Rhonda." Mark thinks Rhonda may fool her male customers for the time being, but in the long run, she will lose them—along with her self-dignity.

───◆───

Professional women in other industries also go to great lengths to close a sale. Julie, a bartender, admits she purposely wears a lingerie blouse when she's behind the bar to reel men in so they'll buy more drinks, ultimately generating more tips. Is this the *smart* way women should do business? Is wearing lingerie that powerful? It's obvious that men enjoy the way women dress. Yet, could you imagine if the tables were turned and a male bartender wore a low-cut shirt while serving drinks? That same strategy seems to have the *opposite* effect on a woman. Women would wonder what he's trying to prove, believe he thinks he's "hot stuff," and are reluctant to give him a tip.

> *"If a woman depends more on her image than her ability, she not only 'sells herself short' but also understates the value that she can bring to the business relationship."*
>
> ~ Jim Mallory, Association Executive, Park Ridge, Illinois

Another example happened recently, when the world came crashing down for the mortgage industry. The wholesalers sub prime loans started going bad in more ways than one. *Business Week Magazine* printed information about the routine frauds, the whistleblowers in several companies, and even the sexual favors behind the fiasco that triggered the global financial crisis.

As the housing bubble was ready to burst, the wholesalers became more aggressive in closing as many loans as possible. Brokers say some female wholesalers weren't up on the finer points of finance, but exploited other assets in their quest to get more loans. "You had boiler rooms of younger, predominantly male brokerage operations and in would walk a gorgeous, fit (wholesaler) who would go desk to desk," said Rick Arvielo, president of New American Funding, a mortgage brokerage in Irvine, California. "Most of them didn't know the product."

Of course, it's acceptable in many industries for companies to hire attractive saleswomen. But in the mortgage business, it went further than usual. The women allegedly offered sexual favors to bank employees. Evan Stone, president of Walnut Creek, California, mortgage brokerage Pacific Union Financial, said that "minimally trained and minimally dressed" wholesalers often wooed brokers. He regularly got visits in his suburban office from representatives wearing unusually short skirts to entice him and his team of brokers to party. Indecent proposals were made—part of building relationships.

Wholesalers also offered sexual favors to co-workers. To drive up their commissions, some enticed loan underwriters at their companies to approve questionable applications. A vice-president at Washington Mutual, who once wielded $500 million to make loans, recalls an incident in which a female wholesaler wanted him to approve a loan that didn't fit the guidelines. The manager, who requested anonymity, says the co-worker, wearing a low-cut shirt, knelt down at his desk and said, "I really need this. What do I have to do?"

All these scenarios are prime examples of women's challenges in the business world. Although selling with sex may bring short-term benefits for some, in the long term, it doesn't lead to true success.

In Susan's example, she did obtain the business, but believed she got it because of her sexy tattoo that was accidentally displayed in front of her potential client. She even received the promotion but didn't think it was well deserved because her sales abilities just did not outshine her butterfly tattoo. Since that day, Susan has felt self-conscious about her tattoo and bandages it when negotiating with a male customer.

As far as Rhonda's arrogant motives go, Mark was right. She eventually lost most of her customers and no longer works for that particular pharmaceutical company. And Julie the bartender has moved on to another job, leaving only memories of her cleavage for the men at the bar. Today, they talk about her in condescending ways one drink after another. Regarding the thousands of wholesalers working the mortgage system, dressing sexually was a norm being swept up in the excitement and excess of a manic market. Then it became time for those women to find a new job.

———◦————

Many women deceive themselves by thinking that the power of lingerie—another analogy for "low-cut dress"—is the best way to get a promotion, make more money, or be awarded the office with the window.

How does this form of deception affect the workplace? Well, the business world still belongs to men, and rightly so because they made it work for themselves. Those women who think the way to take control, be equal, or win the sale by wearing a low-cut dress should watch out! But use of this type of strategy sooner or later backfires. Rumors rumble through the hallways and can damage a woman's reputation for a long time—or even permanently.

> *"Women dressing to impress will find that it backfires when selling a product or service. Many businessmen will be distracted from the sales pitch, discount the presentation as pure hype, or just be turned off."*
>
> ~ Rene A. Henry, Author, *Communicating in a Crisis*, Seattle, Washington

Men have their challenges, too. How they react to the "low-cut dress" can be confusing to them. Few things intimidate men more than an opponent sinking a seemingly impossible 25-foot birdie putt on the golf course; projected sex appeal from a woman is one of them. Whether seen at work, the grocery store, or driving in the next lane, women simply have the power to turn many men into Jell-O (and think of how certain politicians have been caught into this trap). They know this and try to resist it. Instead, many act in embarrassing and unprofessional ways, costing them their reputations if they get caught.

———◦———

Jill is a newly independent contractor who provides supplies to auto body shop owners. From the beginning, she was challenged by this male dominant industry. However, she was determined to win business, especially away from local competitors. Eventually, comments from her customers got back to Jill about the masculine way she dresses every day. Jill was conservative in her way of dress attire. She wore long slacks and a shirt-like blouse and frequently pulled her long brown hair back in a ponytail. She was confronted by a male customer who said, "Jill, haven't you learned yet that if you want my time, you have to wear a skirt? I've told my receptionist that if you come to visit me and you don't have a skirt on, I won't be 'available' to meet with you. Don't waste both our time."

Jill disliked her customer's comment but wore a skirt on her next appointment anyway. But on this visit, the shop owner took his comments too far by saying, "You know, Jill, why don't you just bring me a picture of you so I can stare at you anytime I want, and we don't have to waste our time in these little meetings, especially because I'm not able to move my business referrals over to your company anyway." That was the last appointment Jill made with him. His lack of professionalism in dealing with Jill as a woman may have cost him a better deal than he presently had. It certainly cost him respect from Jill—and probably that of many others.

Like Jill's situation, embarrassing and unprofessional comments by men about women can cause them to lose business. Karen felt uncomfortable when she overheard her doctor remark about how beautiful the Viagra sales representative was—"a 12 on a scale of 1 to 10. She's so good looking," he said, "that no man needs Viagra." Here was Karen's doctor, taking time and attention away from his sick patients to make unprofessional, irrelevant remarks about a sexy woman. She immediately lost respect for him and reported his comment to the front desk manager, who replied, "Oh, that's just the doctor's personality." Apparently, this doctor had the women working in his office under his thumb. Karen wouldn't stand for it; she never returned.

Both men and women need to take responsibility for their behaviors and how they want to be perceived when conducting business together. Wearing a lingerie slip or lacy camisole is a powerful strategy that makes a woman seem more attractive and sexually appealing, and it helps gain attention from men. However, this power may cause miscommunication and isn't advised in a professional setting.

Why? Because when a woman uses the power of lingerie, male prospects wonder if there's something wrong with her service or product, or they question her knowledge and integrity. Is there a flaw in the product itself so the saleswoman feels compelled to use this tactic to draw attention away from it? If so, why would they take such saleswomen seriously?

Sure, most men like it when a woman shows up in a low-cut dress, but they admit it won't close the sale. Such attire not only makes the professional and mature man uncomfortable, it lowers her credibility and can damage her reputation. And if the low-cut dress distracts men, they likely don't make good decisions. They're not thinking with their heads but with their penis.

Instead of drawing attention to their cleavage, women have a better chance of receiving respectful attention if they enhance their best qualities and their finest features, such as their eyes, smile, or manners. Men will notice, remember, and appreciate a woman whose eyes show sincere interest, whose smile is genuine, and whose demeanor is respectful and professional. Read on for many more productive strategies.

———⊰•◦•⊱———

So how do you as a woman decide what to wear to obtain the business that leads to being successful? How can you know that men want to do business in a fair and ethical way? What do you really need to compete in a man's world and how to sell to men without wearing a low-cut dress?

The bottom line is you can profit by selling to men without the superficial, worn-out strategy of dressing seductively and acting provocatively. Believe me, the men represented in this book believe it so. They will tell you that, to be successful, it would be wise to understand who you are and the values of the company you represent.

Forget your high school days of trying to be well-liked and pleasing everyone. Selling is not about being popular; it's about using your skills and talents to the fullest. And it's about being true to yourself no matter what.

Chapter Two

Women Have NOT Come a Long Way, Baby

For centuries, women have been struggling for gender equality.

As much as people want to say women have made great strides, they have to continually prove themselves time and time again. The world still revolves around the male gender, and there's no doubt that men especially dominate the business world.

According to the National Women's Law Center, only 15 of the top 1,500 companies in America are headed by women. On average, women earn 77 cents for every dollar earned by men for the same work. This means that for every $100 she earns, a typical woman has $23 less than men do to spend on rent or mortgage, groceries, household products, child care, and other expenses. It's no wonder women are reaching out to search for other ways that provide more opportunities and advancements, like starting their own businesses.

Men seem to have it easier in life in general. They get to keep their last names; travel with one suitcase; have the same haircut forever; pay less for shirts at the cleaners; don't have to plan the wedding; own maybe two pairs of shoes; are told the truth at car dealerships; get most of the first-class airline seats; don't get pregnant; look "distinguished" with a mustache, wrinkles, and white hair; never have to wear makeup or nylons; don't have the opposite sex staring at their chests; and carry on 10-second phone conversations. It's a fact. Men just have some things easier than women!

On the professional side, our history books prove it's been harder for women to succeed than men. And when they do, sometimes it's difficult for others to accept that they deserve it. The story of Edith Wilson, the wife of Woodrow Wilson, the 28th president of the United States, provides just one example.

Edith is referred to as the first female president of the United States because she secretly took on many of her husband's routine duties and the details of government when President Wilson suffered a serious stroke in 1919. Later, when the truth came out, Edith Wilson was called the "secret president" because she was the first woman to actually run the United States government. *(Source: biography of Edith Bolling Galt Wilson, http://www.whitehouse.gov/history/ firstladies/ew28-2.html)*

Although Mrs. Wilson was commended for her powerful and brave position, leadership would most likely have been different had the secret leaked out sooner. Could it be that she would not have been entrusted with such authority because she was a woman?

Today, women still don't tend to receive equal respect and recognition in business matters. Look at the lack of support for women who want to participate in the workforce but need daycare funding or even maternity leave. As Tracy VanBibber, SVP of sales for Henkel Corporation, stated, "As an executive female in the consumer product goods arena for 24 years, even as far as we've come, there is so much more we need to set our sights on."

Tracy believes there is a way for both gender professionals to succeed. She adds, "We will accomplish this by being articulate, relevant, and finding mutually beneficial, creative solutions. At the end of the day, whether you wear the pants or the skirt, it comes down to who people want to partner with or believe in—to understanding what 'the consumer' needs and delivering the promise better than the man or women next to you."

> *"A woman wearing a low-cut dress to entice a sale is as insulting as a man doing business in a jock strap."*
>
> ~ Ross Shafer, Comedian,
> Ross Shafer Productions,
> Anaheim Hills, California

Why isn't this common sense normal in everyday business dealings?

Saleswomen still feel it takes more effort to prove their self-worth in business and at home than it does for a man. This added pressure makes it extremely challenging to advance in the business world. Women routinely experience high levels of stress every day. "Stress reduction is the number one desire for women today," says Georganne Derick, a home interior designer. "More and more often, women are working, taking care of themselves, a husband, children, and perhaps even elderly parents." Women, in general, are so busy that their voices are simply not heard loudly enough to make a difference, nor are they taken as seriously as they should be. How many times do women bite their tongues and hope for the best?

That's what Tracy VanBibber did. Although a successful

career saleswoman today, Tracy still remembers her earlier experiences trying to advance as a regional manager in Salt Lake City for a $30-plus million dollar consumer product goods company. "I had seven men reporting to me. We were at one of the customer events and our largest revenue customer asked one of the gentlemen who works for me (we will call him Hank), 'Who's the little woman?' My first response was to bury that man with shame because of how he assumed my status was 'the little woman.' But to my surprise, I didn't need to, as Hank pointed out that I had just earned a prestigious sales leadership reward at our company because this 'little woman delivers some of the best results in the company.' After that, there was nothing else for me to say but 'Thank You, Hank.' At least, I know to surround myself with good people that do notice!"

———

The shortage of women in positions of leadership in Fortune 500 companies persists, as Julie Holder, an inspiring, knowledgeable professional, learned all too well. She can confirm that its tough for saleswomen even when the opportunity arises for higher positions as men.

Julie, who was recently promoted to vice president in a prestigious Fortune 500 company, felt proud of this acknowledgement for her hard work. She smiled from ear to ear as she walked through the office hallways. But on the same day her promotion came through, a male executive approached her and said, "I guess its women's promotion week." That insensitive comment poured ice water on her celebration and made her wonder, "Am I being promoted because I'm a woman and not because I'm a great leader?" Even though Julie believes things have gotten better for women, she said, "Women still face stereotypes. We've come a long way, but I wouldn't say we've arrived."

—————

Women aren't innocent bystanders either. Many women generate their own "non-advancement" opportunities as well. For example, many women don't realize that something as simple as applying the low-cut dress strategy actually adds stress to their lives.

According to a *USA Today* study, many women confess they need to dress *provocatively* to get the sale. Also, high-heeled shoes may be fashionable and go with the low-cut dress look, but the extra strain to maintain balance travels up the body, stressing muscles needlessly. Why do women want to harm themselves to be fashionably stressed?

Vickie, known as an extremely high achiever, wanted to be promoted to a national sales position with a destination management company. Early in her career, she received advice to wear high heels every day to give her a powerful image. Vickie bought into believing people judged her by how she looked. This was confirmed in *A Work and Power* magazine survey that showed many women believe they are judged in the workplace on the basis of their looks first, followed by work ethic and accomplishments, then their talent. The same survey indicted men, however, don't believe that dressing provocatively is an important dynamic for the job or closing a sale. Rather, they believe that knowledge, interpersonal skills, and talents are involved in decisions to promote within organizations.

As for Vickie's opportunity to be promoted, the high heels didn't do the trick. She learned it was better to be moderate, appropriate, supportive, and hardworking. To advance in professional status, she now advocates looking polished, with tidy hair, clean teeth, skin, and clothing, and a neutral or fresh body scent. But it's *not* necessary for a woman to add height to her heels.

———————

Many saleswoman shared that selling to men is much harder than selling to women. This is mostly because of communication differences, consumer expectations, and goal-setting standards. Men have a tendency to want different things for different reasons. For example, men have a high regard for gadgets like a remote control while saleswomen think the value of this gadget is minor. However, the male customer likely believes the gadget will make his life easier so he expects the salesperson to show him how the gadget will simplify his life. This communication difference can make or break a sale. Yet, if saleswomen learned how to sell to men and adjust to these difficulties, they'll garner huge profits. They won't get the runaround from men that they do selling to women consumers; they won't get "is it on sale?"; and they won't have to figure out if she is a potentially loyal customer or just window shopping.

"I prefer powerful women, which is even more important to me than their looks or how they dress. Show me you are powerful and know what you are doing, and you have a better chance of making the sale."

~ Stanley Bronstein, CPA, Attorney, Scottsdale, Arizona

Men control the spending of billions of dollars much more than women do and buy for entirely different reasons than women. Take loyalty, for example, and look at how men are loyal with their favorite sports teams. The sports market has proven that men will dig deep into their pockets. The NBA makes $2.2 billion and the NFL $3.3 billion annually—from men buying their favorite team clothing, signs, beer, season tickets and many more. Just in that one market, sports, men offer a lot of sales transactions.

Loyalty can extend to a salesperson, too. There are advantages if serving the customer correctly. Steve, an inspiring young sales manager for a San Francisco hotel, quite often shops at a nearby Nordstrom's department store for shoes. When he's there, he always looks for Carol, his favorite saleswoman, who's 59 and has grandchildren who enjoy sports. Because he's an avid sportsman, it's a natural for him and Carol to talk about sports. As Steve explained, "I'd often wait 30 minutes for Carol to help me. Why? Because she knows I'm a sports maniac, and every time I go into the store to get my shoes shined, she talks to me about my teams-Golden State Warriors and the San Francisco Giants, even though I don't buy shoes from her that day." He added, "Carol is knowledgeable about sports herself so it's fun to get a woman's perspective. The day I do buy shoes from her, she knows what looks good and what's in style and she doesn't try to sell me on her most expensive item, even knowing I can pay the price for it. Most of all, she is there when I'm ready to buy. I can count on her in many ways. If she left her position or the store, I would probably buy somewhere else."

If women can purposefully learn how to sell to men in high positions—like Carol does—they will reap big profits from big sales with the consumers like Steve.

The Hemline Truth

Chapter Three
Women Are Their Own Worst Enemies

Women can be their own worst enemies! Could this be the reason women don't advance at a much faster pace in the business world? Are saleswomen too competitive among themselves? They want the promotion or the corner office with the window or the big sale, but chances are it won't happen if women continue to be their own worst enemies. Men show they believe in other men by working together, promoting each other, cheering each other on, uniting when another man is down. They buy into the motto "all for one, one for all." If men do not experience similar camaraderie from a saleswoman, it's hard for them to want to buy from her.

Women, in general, do not support each other the way it's often perceived. Envy or jealousies make women criticize, judge, and gossip about each other, even engage in "cat fights" as men call them. Women become offended easily and often put themselves in situations that only hinder receiving what they really need or stifle who they really are. Women can be defensive and competitive as they work to claim their own territory and power. They consistently usurp power from each other and actually lose power themselves by these actions. Consequently, no one wins.

> *"The balance of beauty and style is complemented by what's inside, which showcases her true self."*
>
> ~ Tate Hill, Master Colorist/ Hairstylist, Topeka, Kansas

Men have seen how women are rarely supportive of each other. Jeff, a construction worker, hired a 20-year-old woman to be an office assistant. Her first day on the job, she wore a low-cut blouse, mini-skirt, and high-heeled shoes. Other women in the office heard the men's wolf-whistle remarks, but didn't seem to care enough (or may be just plain jealous) to bring them to the young girl's attention. "I don't know what to do," Jeff told his wife. "Her blouse is very revealing, and the workers wear sunglasses so they can look at her without making it so obvious."

Where are the women mentors needed to teach this young lady how to appropriately dress especially in this particular industry?

Even in today's high schools and as early as grade school, girls are competing by wearing the low-cut—well—everything! Jeans, blouses, underwear, shirts, skirts, shorts. Women need to recognize the need to mentor other women, especially inexperienced young ladies who will run organizations in the future.

One of the biggest mistakes saleswomen make in business is to conduct trade-outs and offer service freebies. They may think they are supporting each other and benefiting themselves, but this kind of "business" is actually detrimental to their success. Usually, it involves an exchange in services or products without an exchange of payment.

For example, a saleswoman who provides baby products will give diapers to another saleswomen in exchange for her perfume products with the intention of giving both products exposure. Humbug! Trade-outs do not pay the bills nor count toward making a profit. The only appropriate time to barter or offer freebies is with hobby transactions.

Men, on the other hand, conduct business straight up and then meet in the bar for a cold beer to celebrate their partnership. Women go home and hope the exposure or trade-out pays off some day. Is this any way to conduct business? Is this any way to become successful?

My good friend Michelle recently attended a seminar for women. The female presenter delivered a great message on how women can make millions by going after what they want, telling the group, "Conduct your business like a business. Don't barter or do trade-outs; you must always show your value with your price point." I thought, this seems like a supportive and on-point presentation for women. Then Michelle told me the presenter waived her usual speaking fee for that particular program. Her message declared that "exposure" doesn't pay the bills, but then she contradicted the very point she was presenting! How can she effectively convey a message to other women about making millions of dollars if she doesn't practice what she preaches?

Did I say women can be their own worst enemies?

———⟫•⟪———

When it comes to clothing strategies, women dress certain ways for women as well as for men. In Hollywood, women compete against each other with a vengeance. In business, saleswomen carefully consider how to dress, depending on the customer. As Judy, a highly successful real estate agent, explained, "I would shop for a more feminine dress to wear for a man than I would if I were selling to a woman, subconsciously believing that will score some points for me. As for a woman, I would think she'd become jealous if the way I dress is too feminine and might not give me the sale." Saleswomen actually compete by the way they dress.

Even women in leadership positions have been known to encourage their female sales managers to show some cleavage to attract customers. This can backfire. Sonia, who works for a bank, was told to wear a low-cut dress so when customers approached her window, she would have their attention. Not surprisingly, Sonia became uncomfortable with men always looking at her chest. She confronted her boss (a woman) about it while hoping refusing to do so would not harm her job position. And when top management found out about his strategy, Sonia's boss got demoted. Apparently her boss didn't understand how this strategy makes those who use it look unprofessional. She had put Sonia in a compromised situation.

Saleswomen can be downright evil, too. Sandy, a sales representative for Olay Cosmetics, had traveled to New York on business. She wanted to celebrate her successful trip by going shopping before heading to the airport, so she visited some stores and accumulated several shopping bags with her purchases.

As she entered the last store, she set her bags down and stepped away to view another rack of clothing. The sales clerk picked up the bags and hid them behind the counter, just to see when Sandy would notice. A short while later, Sandy discovered her bags were gone and frantically searched the store. The sales clerk watched her for about 15 minutes before revealing the hidden bags. "Now, don't you feel like a fool?" she admonished Sandy. "You need to watch your items more closely next time." Sandy felt mortified and left the store without buying anything.

In this situation, a positive opportunity for both sales clerk and customer turned sour. Yes, women can be evil to each other!

―――――→•◦•←―――――

The experience of Nina Cash, shows how intelligence, hard work, and coming from the heart win out over beauty. Unfortunately, her story also presents an example of how women can be non-supportive and jealous of each other.

Nina was born in the Philippines a natural, exotic beauty. At age 25, she was recruited to become a model. Her exotic look was in high demand in the 1980s, but coming from a conservative Catholic military family, she knew her parents wouldn't let her start modeling until after her senior year in high school.

Nina Cash

Nina's modeling career after high school provided her the opportunity to be in fashion magazines, catalogs, commercials, and music videos. However, she always knew that modeling was a gift that realistically might not last. Therefore, while working as a model, she continued to attend college and volunteer part-time. After many years of modeling, her interest shifted to education.

While volunteering for the Special Olympics, Nina had the opportunity to engage with children of various disabilities including autism and Down syndrome. Nina passionately loved teaching and working with these kids. In fact, Nina had an "ah ha" moment when she realized she wasn't in their lives to teach *them*, but they were in her life to teach *her*. The children's smiles and true love of life warmed Nina's heart and changed her perspective.

Soon after she started with the Special Olympics, Nina began working with a vocational special education program for a school district. Her main duty involved developing jobs for high school seniors with developmental disabilities. So she conducted sales calls to companies and successfully placed her students into jobs. What was the secret to her success? She was honest, had integrity, and could sell from her heart.

When Nina changed jobs, she stayed in the workforce development field. It wasn't until she turned 30 that she had difficultly proving her self-worth. Her beauty, more than her skills and knowledge, challenged other saleswomen. She worked in the staffing industry and continued to sell from the heart, but the human resources department began receiving complaints about her. The staff of women accused Nina of using her beauty and modeling status to advance.

This hurt Nina terribly. On top of it, men curiously asked, "Who is this chick?" Some men even offered her promotions if she would spend time with them beyond office hours. Nina certainly was not interested. She constantly was in a position to keep proving herself over and over, but she never gave up. Her family and friends provided a wonderful support system, giving her strength and guidance.

Nina continued to educate herself and apply her talents to the best of her abilities while ignoring the complaints. Soon, her focus on education paid off. She was approached by a university to work in the corporate education department as director. She blossomed, going above and beyond to help others. They began to call her the CCO (chief connectivity officer) because, if she couldn't help someone, she'd find a person who could. What a great way for Nina to deflect complaints about her using her beauty!

Today in her mid-40s, Nina still "knocks your socks off" with her beauty. But beyond that, she knows what it takes to be successful. She made sure her honesty, integrity, knowledge, skills, and strong work ethic outshone her appearance. Nina feels that is the way to know how to sell to men too.

According to Saurage Research, 7 in 10 women bosses say they have to work harder and be smarter than men just to get the same respect in the workplace. Men agree that women need to do more to get equal respect. It's up to women to turn this statistic around by showing full respect for each other.

Nina Cash offers 10 tips to help women get started.

Nina's 10 Tips for Saleswomen

1. Always have a support system of family and friends in place. Surround yourself with people who will guide you and keep you grounded. Be open to hear what others see from a different perspective.

2. Don't do unfavorable things just to get promoted. Your bad karma will haunt you!

3. Never define who you are by the job title you hold. Be humble and grateful.

4. Volunteer and share your talents and skills with others. Chances are, good things will come from it.

5. Honesty, ethics, and integrity should guide your behavior and decisions. Your reputation tells others who you are.

6. Be happy with yourself. If you are truly happy with yourself, it will be apparent to others and possibly contagious.

7. No matter what the situation is, always be on good terms with others. We've heard this a million times before, and it is 100% true. NEVER burn bridges and always be gracious.

8. Discover optional ways to be successful. Be open to opportunities. You might lose a few battles but end up winning the war. So, instead of fighting off something you have no control over, try embracing it to see what happens. There is a reason for everything.

9. Be beautiful on your own terms. Define what beautiful means to you in ways that others will feel the same.

10. Always be confident without being arrogant and pompous.

When it comes to being competitive, be in what I call "co-opetition" with other women. Choose to partner and meet or exceed goals together because not all women are evil or non-supportive. Some women cheer and applaud other women. Some women do great things for each other.

Billie Jean King, the great tennis champion and author of
Pressure Is a Privilege, is a highly accomplished business
woman and an long-time friend of my family. Billie Jean said,
"We have a responsibility to help other women. Each
generation stands on the shoulders of those who came before
them. I was fortunate and blessed to achieve fame. But if I
don't use the opportunities that have come to me because of
my fame to help others, I am missing an opportunity for me
and for others."

Billie Jean truly lived her promise when my mother, Ruth
Ann, was working for her on the tennis circuit years ago.
Mom recalled a time when Billie Jean had invited her over
to her Chicago apartment. Billie Jean shared confidences
with Mom and
showed her
some of her
first trophies.
She told Mom
about wanting
to enter her first
tournament but
she didn't have
the money. A
friend stepped
in to make it
possible and

Billie Jean King with Ruth Ann Gardner

Billie Jean actually won the tournament. Then, as they toured
her apartment, Billie Jean showed my mom a huge closet full
of clothes collected from around the world and invited her to
pick whatever she'd like to take home for a souvenir.

My mom was overwhelmed by Billie Jean's generosity. Here
was a rising young tennis star who, at one time, had nothing.

She'd become one of the most famous athletes in the world, and was giving her clothes away to other women for no special reason other than Billie Jean enjoyed giving.

Like Billie Jean, I believe women need to come together—and to get rid of any power struggles between each other. But, instead stand tall while empowering women to victory. They need to stand up for their convictions and support each other in matters of equal rights, recognition, loyalty, needs, love, sisterhood, promotions. Yes, women are continuing to figure out how they can believe in themselves and still believe in other women. Billie Jean King does it—why can't we all?

> *"A woman in a low-cut dress compromises her true sense of business and ethics. I question what she is really trying to sell me ... Can she be trusted, is she honest, and is she ethical?"*
>
> ~ Jaimie Mattes, Regional Director, Helms Briscoe, Minneapolis, Minnesota

In contrast, men generally support each other. Take, for example, San Francisco Giants' baseball great Barry Bonds. Many men wish they could hit a baseball just like Barry. I've heard men badmouth him when he didn't get the home run needed to win a game, but they still support him. Although Barry Bonds may not be perfect, men still believe he's the greatest player ever because they would love to have his percentages just in their own men's baseball game leagues.

It's the same in business. Men may laugh at Donald Trump's or Bill Gate's hairdos, but given the opportunity, many would drop their jobs in a minute to be as successful as they are. Men can argue about any subject, but they admit that Barry

Bonds, Donald Trump, and Bill Gates are among the best in their fields. That's why I think men see "the better side" of other men and are supportive of each other's skills.

Think of how far women could go if they supported each other to the best of their abilities. Consider the beauty pageants like Miss America or Miss USA in which quality women participate to be declared "the best." They showcase their potential to someday be doctors, lawyers, police officers, or whatever they wish. Their universal hope is for greater fulfillment and a better world.

Yes, women enter these pageants to help themselves succeed. And what does the public tend to do? Knock them down. Women have been known to boycott watching pageants on television (unless a sister or friend has entered in the contest) because they say pageants aren't "good" for women. Just because the main concept behind pageants is "beauty," women jealously declare these events shallow. They show little or no support for the young ladies working hard to be successful in this way. Do you see how women hold each other back, even in simple contests?

Although support is important to have, another's jealousy need not hold women back from advancement. In fact, jealousy is more harmful to those harboring such feelings. The best way to conquer jealousy is to honestly compliment other women. Men compliment other men all the time. As Miguel Munquia, a convention center sales manager, said, "Guys have more security than women when it comes to compliments. We say things like, 'hey man, cool car, great football pass, nice tie, or sweet golf swing, dude.' We even give compliments by patting each other on the butt.

Women just stare at each other from across the room with envy on their faces." Miguel's point is that women need to rethink their behavior, for it ultimately benefits them to give compliments. It could be as simple as saying, "I'm happy for you" when something good happens. Imagine the lasting friendships and possible business that could result. Besides that, it simply feels good to compliment others.

————

The challenge remains. How can women, especially saleswomen, control their own destinies? As a woman, you embody a powerful realism. It's up to you to compliment others, to be stronger than ever, to face challenges that arise, to celebrate successes for yourself and for each other. The key is to be consistently respectful toward other women in business—women of color, women from different industries. Support each other, whether it be your mother, sister, co-worker, neighbor, or a stranger soon to become a friend. Support for each other will make women more powerful and successful.

Of course, you may not always agree with another woman, but strive to see life from her viewpoint. Learn about her business, know your business well, and compare them. You never know how you might be able to work together, to support each other, to cheer each other on to success. Mostly, by pulling together with others, you'll enhance your own power.

Respect those who have earned it. You'll know when a woman deserves a pat on the back, so give it to her. And guess what? Men will notice how women show their respect for each other, too.

Chapter Four
What Women Need To Know About Sales

"What's the difference between a
hockey mom and a pit bull? – Lipstick!"

~ Sarah Palin, 2008 U.S. Vice Presidential Candidate

The sales world is tough, complicated, and highly competitive. According to Manpower, Inc., sales jobs are among the top five most difficult job categories to fill, along with engineers, machinists, skilled trades, and technicians. Selling is the act of persuading a customer or client to buy a product or service—and this takes skill. Not only that, but ideally buyers are happy with what they've been sold.

To sell is to serve, no matter who your customer is. It should be a winning situation between a buyer and a seller, but all too often, it isn't. If the sales process were always based on principles with fair intentions, everyone would likely be satisfied in the end. But principles seem to get lost somewhere along the line.

Knowing how to serve and negotiate a mutually beneficial outcome are just two skills required for sales. Another is exemplified by Sarah Palin, the 2008 Republican vice presidential candidate. No matter who you voted for in that election, if you're a saleswoman, you can relate to Sarah Palin in that she's competing in a man's world and selling the American people on her "true self." Sarah seemingly came out of "nowhere," yet was chosen to be a vice presidential candidate. How did she do it? Confidence! Sarah Palin stood up for what she believed in as well as her knowledge and experience. She took her confidence to greater heights than anyone could have imagined and accepted the challenge to run just weeks before the election.

Yes, she was considered by some to lack skills and talents necessary for such a high office. Yes, she was judged by the amount of money her campaign spent on her clothing. But, by golly, she fought for what she believed in—herself and her ideas. Now, that's confidence! Sarah's determination and expression of her truth can inspire all women to build confidence in themselves.

———

How do women become confident? Where does belief and understanding of oneself come from? Well, first let's look at where it *doesn't* come from.

Early in life, many women were considered "daddy's little girls" and taught to dress in pretty colors, sit like little ladies, and talk when spoken to. They often grew up to follow someone else's vision of who they should be instead of naturally developing their own interests and talents. Most women didn't have the opportunity to learn new skills, apply their talents, or gain the knowledge to become their own leaders. The entrepreneurial dream for women has been a challenging vision for some and nowhere in sight for others, until now.

So how do "daddy's little girls" build the kind of confidence Sarah Palin exudes? How do women make the transition from having no confidence to being highly confident in the profession of sales?

They *learn* confidence. "Learned confidence" is developed in the same way sales skills and techniques are learned. They're put into action and eventually get translated into belief in oneself. Skills such as communication and negotiation can also be learned, but have to be used consistently. This is why women need to practice, because when they do, they're *doing* something. Practice improves performance, and performance improves sales.

Confidence is about being deeply rooted in unwavering self-belief that feels natural and comfortable. Feeling confident means being sure of your skills to succeed in a task or goal. In other words, confidence is born by demonstrating your sales abilities. It's an internal judgment based on your own track record. It's also about you and how you're determined to accomplish what you want. Many women lack the ability to develop confidence, understand it, or use it to their advantage. They often feel everyone *else* has it—not them.

Above all, confidence is a *perception*. And perception can become reality—unless it's been distorted. For example, many women have the perception that when they wear a low-cut dress (or its suggestive equivalent), they will get what they're striving for. In reality, this demeanor displays a *lack* of confidence in their skills and knowledge. Even if they do achieve accomplishments, the underlying truth is that it happened because of wearing the low-cut dress. From there, it may cause other lack-of-confidence traits. Maybe it puts down their achievements by saying something like, "Oh, it wasn't a big deal" or "I was just lucky." Lack of confidence also shows up when someone takes on a task or goal that is way too much—not a good feeling for anyone to experience when she wants to boost her confidence. It is important to understand and be clear on how perception plays a big part to being confident.

―――⇒›‹⇐―――

The biggest *mis*perception for women in the business world is fear, or False Expression Appearing Real. Fear can affect saleswomen in many situations, from having to give their opinions to conducting sales presentations, to not asking for the business. With consistent fear, hesitation, or lack of confidence, their way of thinking develops into an attitude, and when fear plays a part, that attitude is negative. This negative attitude will then detract from their performance. They are better off being honest and take action to conquer the fear, a characteristic that builds confidence.

For example, while Eric was traveling on business, he wanted to try a new restaurant in town. He met up with friends there for dinner and noticed ribs on the menu—his favorite. Eric asked the waitress, "How are the ribs tonight?" The waitress answered with honest, "The ribs are alright, but the steak is great." Due to the waitress's confidence in sharing her opinion with her customer, she had created a better result for both of them, Eric was extremely pleased with his steak and gave the waitress a bigger tip than he might have otherwise.

―――⇒›‹⇐―――

Another fear saleswomen have is being perceived as a bitch, a description conferred on women all too often, usually because of warped perspectives. Can a woman who is "too confident" come across as a bitch? Well, it's not the first time a woman has been classified this way.

Pamela, a hotel sales professional, had an experience of being perceived as a bitch early in her career. An intelligent business woman, she's always aware of her surroundings, including how she dresses in the office. However, it had been a challenge to find a dress that fits both her small chest and healthy-sized thighs. She recalled wearing a beautiful blue silk dress that buttons down the front. However, when she wore that dress, she had to be careful bending over because the gap between the buttons revealed her bra.

One day, Pamela caught John, one of the sales managers, talking to her chest instead of her face. He wouldn't look her in the eyes. Later, in a colleague's office, Pamela shared her frustration about John by saying, "The next time he does that, I'll stare at his crotch." They both laughed and shook their heads, not believing it would happen.

The next thing they knew, John walked into the office and again started to talk to her chest. So Pamela, a woman of her word, stared at John's crotch while she talked to him. No lie! Immediately flustered, John retorted, "Hey, bitch, what are you doing!?"

"If you want to talk to my chest, I'll talk to your crotch!"

This direct response shocked John. From that day forward, he showed complete respect for Pamela. She gained confidence having followed through on her convictions. And the next day, she gave away the dress to get rid of all the negative vibes from that experience.

⟫◦⟪

There are many ways women are considered as a bitch. Sometimes a woman might be labeled a bitch because she talks "too much." Sure, women can talk a lot, but so what?

A talkative woman is a good thing in sales, as long as she's offering pertinent information. Sometimes telling the truth is seen as bitchy too.

Marsha and David, who work for a California winery that produces fine wines, are quite competitive with their sales quotas. Marsha liked to talk a lot while David is much more reserved. They both were given travel budgets for when they exhibited their wine samples out of town. Halfway through the year, the reports showed that Marsha had stayed within her budget but David had already exceeded his. So at the next company sales meeting, Marsha took it upon herself to report on the midyear budget. She made it clear she was more competent than David when it came to travel expenditures. Later, she heard others say she was just a bitch. This didn't bother Marsha; she believed in stating the facts truthfully. She also knew she wasn't the one taking advantage of the company budget.

> *"The old saying is that 'sex sells.' If that's true, then consider the sexiest thing that anyone can display—confidence. A woman who is confident in who she is and what she's doing and doesn't have to resort to showing skin to sell—that's sexy in the best sense of the word."*
>
> ~ Joe Calloway, Speaker, Author, *Work Like You're Showing Off!* Nashville, Tennessee

Marsha is to be congratulated for standing up for what she believed was right, both for herself and the company. It's what's called the new ROI—Return On "I." This reflects how saleswomen can take advantage of ways to stay above the competition, especially in a man's world, while doing it with integrity as well.

Every woman who controls a situation like Marsha did, risks being labeled a "bitch." You may think you're not "controlling" at times when you are, for your actions and decisions affect others in ways they don't like it. But accept that it's okay to be a "bitch." You have the capability to be straightforward and confident, and to control situations—and rightly so when it comes to your own ROI.

⸺➤◦◄⸺

To face your fears and boost your confidence, it's also important to believe in your performance and trust yourself. David Selley, with Target Management Services, said, "Unfortunately, women have a lot more at stake emotionally in the trust department than men. Women are nourishing and security oriented. Men are gatherers and hunters by nature. Therefore, there is a perception that women have been robbed of lifelong tools that men have been given. Men can sense a woman's confidence level by how she trusts, believes in, and values herself. So, it's up to the power of women who are inspired and ready to get rid of that perception."

Exactly what can you do to gain confidence? Try these ideas: Write a journal to track your thoughts, opinions, viewpoints, fears, wants, and needs. Make a point of acknowledging your accomplishments in your journal—and share them with others. The next time you lose weight or make a big sale or are involved with a charity event, tell everyone how you did it. Celebrate in a way that is fun for you. You deserve to acknowledge yourself. This self-acknowledgement, when performed regularly, will help build your self-confidence.

All of these are good, but the primary confidence builder is knowledge. No matter what the perception, the experience or the purpose, having knowledge makes you an expert who knows your business, products, and/or services well. And with knowledge, you receive an automatic boost in confidence, which transfers to customers and results in sales.

Sound easy? It is, as long as you keep learning. Focus on your interests and passions, then knowledge will follow, as you will naturally want to learn about them. Take responsibility to read books, talk to people, do research, and explore areas of interest to better yourself. Make a firm decision to become more knowledgeable tomorrow than you are today.

Diana Don Colby, director of financial education at a leading financial services company Capital One, said commonly, women are challenged just to buy a car. "It's troubling to see that women still do not feel empowered to manage the car-buying process on their own. It's important for them to realize that confidence and purchasing power require education—not a male companion. Rather than turning to a man for support, women should instead take advantage of the variety of educational resources available to them."

When selling to men, applying your confidence in a style that works can be learned. If you "ready, aim, fire" in a direct way, men will respond. After all, a good solution is a man's top criterion for buying. In contrast, women need comfort, affirmations, and a friendly approach throughout the sales process. Thus a woman-to-woman sale transaction tends to take longer than when men are involved.

Here's an example of using a pushy style that didn't work. Recently, I received a phone call from a radio station selling advertising spots. Only 10 seconds into her sales pitch, the saleswoman asked for my credit card number. I was shocked. I needed to hear more about the offer and think about it for a few days. As a potential customer, I found her approach too cold, too fast, and too direct. Plus it added way too much pressure to my personal buying process.

This proved to be a poor sales strategy for selling to a potential woman customer. She didn't take the time to find out about my company and if my business was right for her market. Plus, her style made me feel uncomfortable. It would have been better if she'd recognized that, as a woman, I wanted to hear the complete offer and think about it before giving her my decision. If the sales woman used this approach on a male consumer, she would have had a better chance at closing the sale. Yet, she still needed to be careful not to incorporate too many hard-sell techniques. Understanding the differences between how the two genders prefer to be approached would have made her sales presentation more effective.

Irma, an international airline sales representative, learned how to do just that, although it was a rough process. In the early 1990s, Irma worked in a male-dominated office of 13 men, handling accounts that were headed by men. Due to gender and cultural differences, Irma learned early on to trust her knowledge in this environment. She worked hard and achieved her sales goals yearly.

One day, Irma's boss, Rick, heard disturbing rumors about her. They implied that Irma had been spending too much time beyond office hours with her customers in order to close sales. Shocked by this allegation, she wanted to convey her side of the story. So to respond to Rick's claim, she invited him to dinner with a client to prove how she achieves her goals. What Rick didn't know is that Irma always invited her client's spouse, too.

Their dinner with the couple went well, and Irma was able to get a contract signed right on the spot at the restaurant. Then the client and his wife invited Irma to their home for dinner the following week to celebrate. In this "over and above" step of the sales process, she got to meet their kids, see how the family lives, and continue the relationship. This happened as a result of her building client relationships that included wives. And Rick witnessed it firsthand.

Irma proved that women can be influential and effective while becoming the "expert" on a customer's needs. This process has paid off well despite the jealousy and rumors from her colleagues. Irma took her knowledge a step further by encouraging other women to become experts and find ways to go "above and beyond" the usual expectations.

No matter what circumstances or situations arise, you can control your confidence the way you control your attitude and professionalism. It's a learned skill that constantly needs your attention. And it's great when it gets a boost!

I recently attended a Hyatt Hotel customer appreciation event, which took place at the Pole Position Raceway in Las Vegas. It was exhilarating because of the fast pace of activities in which everyone participated. As a sports enthusiast, I was especially thrilled to meet the famous race car driver, Al Unser Jr.—an approachable and friendly guy.

As I felt my confidence build in this setting, I put myself to the test by challenging him to a race. Much to my surprise, Al immediately accepted and started to help me with my gear. My heart started to race first—before I even put my foot to the pedal! Then hesitation kicked in. I thought, *What did I just do? Could I really race against the best race car driver in the world?* Granted, we weren't on a real racetrack; we were in his backyard on his own private racetrack. But still, could I really race against Al Unser Jr. and not embarrass myself in front of my customers?

Well, Al being a gentleman did offer me a seven-second head start, just to be fair. Fair? I wanted to compete against him on an "equal" basis. But Al thought his offer was fair because, after

Deborah with Al Unser Jr.

all, he had been racing professionally for years while I have only raced around the neighborhood on my bicycle as a small child. Then, all of a sudden, all I could think about was winning so I could tell the entire world I beat Al Unser Jr.!

Okay, I needed to wake up to reality. So I accepted his offer of a seven-second head start. As the crowd gathered to cheer, I began visualizing the race I was about to win. Then I heard the starter say, "Drivers, start your engines." I placed the heavy helmet on my head, we gave each other the respectful thumbs up, the starter's flag dropped, and I began the twelve-lap race with fury using my seven-second head start.

Of course, predictably Al caught up to me. It was all in fun. But truth be known, when we raced across the finish line, I actually won—well, given the seven-second spread. Al Unser Jr. graciously signed my scorecard, which read, "Deborah, winner in a seven-second spread."

Can women win against a man in a sporting event? You bet! After all, our family friend Billie Jean King won against Bobby Riggs in the "Battle of the Sexes" tennis match on September 20, 1973. And now, I had won against Al Unser Jr. I still talk about this incredible experience racing against him. Believing in my performance with confidence helped me win fair and square. It could have been an uncomfortable and embarrassing situation, but it ended up as a success that I can gloat about. I had willingly taken a risk that made the experience all worthwhile. Transformations to success like this can happen to everyone.

Top performers consistently challenge and believe in themselves. They are competitive people who keep moving forward by learning and noticing the positive stance they can take in every situation. They understand and accept competition. They regard it as healthy, fun, and exhilarating while handling any fearful situations with poise. They are motivated, inspired, and in control. When fear becomes an obstacle, confident performers turn the situation into a positive experience while finding ways to overcome the obstacle.

———≫•≪———

Nothing is impossible. You have to dream big. You have to deliberately set high goals for yourself. Develop belief in your own performance that requires action. You can conquer any challenge or obstacle at work, at home, and at play if you believe in yourself and know you have the power to be confident. Take control of the circumstances and situations around you. One strategy is to increase your confidence is by self-talk. Practicing this will help you increase your sales because your ability to project self-confidence makes the difference between a sale and a walk-away situation with your customers. How will you know when you have obtained confidence? By repeatedly accepting and acknowledging your achievements, just say, "I can do this." Become a master in confidence! It will make you successful.

Become Confident

Just practice the following actions to achieve "learned confidence." They are simple to apply—even when selling to men.

How to Have Learned Confidence

- Acknowledge your fears.
- Let go of the past.

- Stop judging yourself.
- Start focusing and listening to yourself.
- Commit to making adjustments.

How to Have More Learned Confidence

- Think "self-development."
- Set goals/write a journal.
- Be prepared to work hard.
- Keep learning.
- Pay attention.

How to Have Even More Learned Confidence

- Act successfully.
- Learn how to give and take.
- Have pride in YOU.
- Always smile.
- Congratulate yourself!

Winning Over The Male Customer

Chapter Five
Gender *Does* Matter in Sales

Now that you understand the importance of becoming an expert with confidence, you're ready to learn how to increase your sales by selling to men. However, the first step is to get into the new mindset of "flipping your focus" as a saleswoman. This does not mean ignoring female consumers; they are good customers too, although they expect more choices, more services, more options, and more time to decide. They want respect, communication, and appreciation for their business, and can sometimes be bitchy when they don't get what they want.

Yes, women customers can be high maintenance—especially when it comes to the decision factor. According to *Prevention Magazine*, on average, women make decisions 70 percent more slowly than men. This means women don't really know what they want when it comes to being a buyer during the purchase process. I know … I am one!

As a female buyer, when someone tries to sell something to me such as jewelry, I'm skeptical and ask questions like "Is this jewelry real or not? Is it over-priced? Under priced? Worth purchasing? Will it match my new outfit?" I take my time and do my research looking for a better deal. Same scenario when I'm researching airfares on the Internet. I look for hours, sometimes days, on the sites that offer the best airfares or flight times; I even call my friends or a travel agent to get more information. I do whatever I can to get the airfare in my price range or work with my preferred airline. All this work seems to be worth it—especially when I have to explain my decision. The bonus is telling others about the best deal I just secured.

Most women I know have similar high-maintenance traits. Women shopping at the malls are always looking for the best bargain. Watch them as they go through the stores mall from one end to the other, and then walk back through the ones that attracted them to make a purchase—maybe.

As I said, women buyers are generally high maintenance, so as a saleswoman, why spend all your time and energy pursuing their business? Instead "flip your focus" by taking a closer look at customers who are likely to provide more loyalty and greater profits—men!

That requires taking relationships with men more seriously than ever. Building good relationships is already important to women, which gives saleswomen a good start in the sales process. Research has helped determine the fundamental difference between men and women, and how it affects the sales process. From a young age, consider the diversity of communication, memory, and emotions. As Marshall Brian, author of *The Teenager's Guide to the Real World*, wrote: "In general, men are much more aggressive than women, while women tend to be more social. Men tend to rely more on rational thought while women rely more on feelings. These observations are generalizations, of course, but fairly obvious. You can see these tendencies in children at play. Girls play with dolls and work with each other socially, while boys wage mock wars with one another. It is important to recognize that neither sex is 'better.' They are simply wildly different."

Research by Dr. Jonathan M. Psenka, a naturopathic physician, noted that differences like male and female hormone levels contribute to differing stress responses *(http://www.4wecare.com)*. It indicates that women don't have testosterone levels that are as high as those found in men. (Testosterone is an anabolic steroid associated with increased muscle mass, hair growth, and aggression.) Having increased levels of testosterone—combined with a brain that is 'wired' for more anxiety-like stress responses like what scientists find through magnetic resonance imaging (MRI)—might explain why men respond differently to certain sales techniques compared to women. The MRI technique uses radio waves to measure changes in the body. MRIs can identify changes such as oxygen consumption, blood vessel dilation/contraction, and organ responses to chemical events in the body.

> *"Women who wear a low-cut dress in a professional setting are unacceptable and improper. What's the underlying message? I don't trust them and what they are trying to sell to me."*
>
> ~ John Springrose, AIG, Chicago, Illinois

So, if a man feels pressured to buy a product or service, typically he experiences increased stress that causes him to make a negative and possibly a regrettable decision. For example, a contract deadline that needs to be met and a saleswoman that wants her customer's signature to confirm. The man will feel either motivated or frustrated in this situation. Signing a contract has to be beneficial for him; he needs a compelling reason to sign it. He may still feel pressure, but it's a good motivational stress. Alternatively, he can feel frustrated. This is where an MRI would show a fight-

or-flight response causing increased production of hormones associated with acute danger and anxiety. As a salesperson, the best way to handle your customer's frustration pressures is to step away and allow him to decide on his own time. Knowing and accepting gender differences can make you more alert in any situation, including selling to men.

Tell me, in the business world, who is making most of the buying decisions? What decisions are being made by those earning the most dollars in the workplace? And who has higher-ranked positions and makes more pay? Yep, you guessed it—*men!*

Even when buying homes, men tend to make the final decisions. Marketing guru Doris Pearlmen said, "Men tend to be linear thinkers and approach the home-buying process as a matter-of-fact business deal. On the other hand, women are more relationship-driven, and when making a big purchase like a new home, women are more likely to want to discuss the process with others, including friends and family. They like to run ideas back and forth with others. By then, the men have already made a decision."

New statistics are being generated as male consumers evolve. According to *Men's Magazine*, the U.S. male population has topped 105 million. This statistic is predicted to increase 9.2 percent in just a few short years, which is much faster than the female population is expected to increase. Although overall buying power used to be measured by market size between genders, the male buying market is expected to grow nearly 32 percent by 2012. This growth is due to the emerging diverse male consumer, with the most buying impact coming from the 25 to 49 age bracket. From the interviews conducted with more than 400 diverse men, collectively they spend a total of approximately $4 billion per year on personal and professional expenditures. Those expenditures include office items, software products, family vacations, personal hygiene items, and more. It's just another reason for saleswomen to "flip their focus" to male consumers, who constitute today's buying power.

So, it makes me wonder: If men are considered to rule the biggest purchases, why haven't saleswomen learned to focus their efforts on selling to male consumers?

Well, although this is good news for saleswomen, the payoff to switch to the male consumer may not be all that easy to accomplish. Men judge saleswomen's professionalism by their appearance. This not only includes how they dress but how they walk and how they wear their hair and make-up. The entire package is important to them. When a saleswoman walks into a man's office, he knows immediately if he wants to do business with her. The majority of the time, he can tell by the way she presents herself—a frequent topic of conversation among men. Unfortunately, women hear about those conversations but don't take them seriously. Saleswomen, take heed. Be careful to present yourselves in a polished manner in selling situations.

Additionally, to gain an edge, you might consider living in a city that has the greatest opportunity to sell to men. A *Business Journal* study that focused on the nation's 100 largest metropolitan areas ranked the San Francisco-Oakland area, Washington, and New York City as the most female-friendly. Los Angeles, Madison (Wisconsin), Boston, and Denver follow.

What about flipping your focus? As a woman, you know how to nurture and care for others. Men will pay attention to you if you display that nurturing and caring instinct you have when you are conducting business. Take the analogy of cooking. Women care how a meal is prepared. Once a recipe becomes familiar, they add their own flavors, sauces, or spices to make the meal special.

It's the same idea when servicing male buyers. Watch the popular Emerald cooking show in which the host says "Bam!" and tosses that extra "tender loving care" of spice into the cooking pot. Or how about Paula Deen's home cooking show? As she says in her southern drawl, "It's the quality of the ingredients that makes the quality."

Similarly, if you deliver extra care throughout your sales efforts, men will appreciate you, become repeat customers, and/or they will refer you to other male potential customers.

Overall, men don't receive enough credit as being good customers. As a saleswoman, you can reap the benefits of selling to men, largely because they quickly know what they want and tell the truth upfront. Purchasing a product or receiving a service is not even about power for them. Have you ever heard of an "All Male Power Conference?" No, because men don't need to feel their power when it comes to this buying process. They simply listen, decide, and move on. Yes, men do lean on each other for referrals, but only if it doesn't take too much time, if they're needed and in subtle ways. Generally, they know what they want, so it's a matter of finding out what that is by providing the right answers.

> *"A business woman who wears a low-cut dress walks down a divided highway."*
>
> ~ David H Selley, Author,
> *Health Wealth & Happiness,*
> Los Angeles, California

Gender differences, roles, and relationships are significantly affecting consumer behavior. The position of men is changing in the workplace, as are their relationships with women and their involvement in family life. For example, more married men are taking on child-rearing and household chores traditionally handled by women. As this happens, assumptions about the participation of men in family purchases are changing.

According to Phil Goodman with Genergraphics, which offers generational marketing services, men still earn much higher income than women, and especially divorced men (paying only alimony, if any) and Gen X men (who either work hard for their money or have been given family inheritances). Right now, high-paying occupations are dominated by men, with 27 million men earning $50K or more and nearly 5.8 million men earning at least $100K. A significant number of men live as same-sex couples, which often means a household with two higher-paying occupations. Are you starting to see dollar signs from these potential male customers? (See www.genergraphics.com for more information.)

When shopping, a vast difference in the way men and women behave has been studied. The U.S. Men's Market research and Packaged Facts, a division of MarketResearch.com (see www.marketresearch.com) shows that although men view themselves as "buyers," they are generally considered to be spontaneous buyers and not window shoppers like most women. So, when they approach the seller for a product or service, it's best to quickly figure out the details to close the sale because chances are they're ready to buy.

The following are key characteristics of the typical male consumer:

- Men shop when they "have" to; women shop because they "want" to.

- Men are primary shoppers in one out of five households and are not interested in sales or specials.

- Men do more grocery shopping than ever before, but grocery stores are still designed for women.

- Men shop for brand names, which are more expensive than generic items.

- Younger generational men like to shop for fashions that will make them popular with their friends or girlfriends.

- Boomer men's buying patterns have been transformed by Internet purchasing possibilities. They buy more then they used to due to online options.

- Men most likely see shopping as a family activity, especially in the southern regions

- Men with fashion brand awareness and interest in personal care products are concentrated in metro areas (like New York City).

- Men are prime customers for new electronics and home products.

- Today's full-time dads are more involved with their families and spend more on their children than ever.

- Single men between ages 22 and 25 total over 37 million in the U.S., and their average after-tax income is as high as $69,000.

- Men walk into an auto mall lot 10 to 15 times more often than women.

Due to these findings, various media are taking a different look at the male consumer. In the past, marketers developed a message, then determined the appropriate media channel (e.g., TV, radio, magazines, Internet). Today, marketers first determine what market segment a media channel addresses (e.g., young men, middle-aged women, teenage girls ...) and then develop a message for that channel that relates to that market segment. Marketers are learning about their preferences through questionnaires that spell out what magazines they read, what they search for using Internet search engines, what they write in blogs, which websites they visit, and what they say in online reviews.

Bazaarvoice, a research firm, offers product and service ratings for customers to review. Its research shows men prefer to search for answers themselves, and 80 percent of men consider Bazaarvoice to be an important resource. *(See www.bazaarvoice.com for more information.)* One discovery Bazaarvoice made is that the younger generational males actually look for magazines that focus on shopping. Another is that they prefer to watch sports on the Internet, although it's still highly popular for men to watch sports events on television or listen on the radio. The older generational males will watch or listen to news and talk shows while the younger generational males prefer listening to music. As a saleswomen, think how your products or services may be advertised or promoted to attract your target markets.

The media have implemented successful marketing campaigns for certain male market segments, such as Nivea lotion for dry-skinned men, Burger King products aimed at young men who spend time on the Internet, and Coke or Pepsi, which attract diet-conscious men. To attract the older generational male consumer (a quickly expanding group), Nintendo is taking new approaches that will pique interest with games they are already familiar with. The Gap is changing clothing styles to better fit different body types of all ages.

Many other research firms realize the importance of the "forgotten" male consumer. The NPD Group, Inc. *(see www. ndp.com)*, a leading provider of consumer and retail research data, announced the launch of its tracking service for the men's active apparel business for U.S. sporting goods retailers to help direct their purchases. "By launching this new service, NPD is able to develop a highly focused view of the men's active apparel market in sporting goods retailers and, for the first time, provide key insights into what we now know to be a $1.9 billion dollar market," stated Dennis Brown, president of The NPD Group, Inc. "The point-of-sale data in combination with NPD's consumer insights will make a valuable contribution to the retailers understanding the men's active apparel business."

NPD has been successfully tracking prestige fragrances for men as well. For the first time in the last decade, a men's fragrance scored the top spot as the new launch product for all fragrances with Sean "Diddy" Combs's Unforgivable scent. Accomplishments of Unforgivable speaks to a large sales opportunity in men's fragrances. And Prestige, another men's scent, was the top-selling fragrance for 9 out of 12 months.

———◦◦◦———

Saleswomen need to be aware of these trends and ideas to attract the male consumer. Also, be aware of the fact that men are competitive when it comes to their buying habits. Yes, men do compliment each other, but underneath the camaraderie, they have a competitive streak toward each other. They may not admit it, but be attentive to this common behavior. If a friend or co-worker says he just bought a big-screen television or a new car over the weekend, you can bet his buddy will go out and buy one too—or at least want to. Listen to their conversations and be prepared if your products and services provide a good fit.

———»·0·«———

Gender *does* matter in sales. As stated earlier, the best thing you can do is to build relationships with potential male clients and learn how to apply relationship-building to winning their business. How? First, make sure you know and apply the fundamentals of selling. It doesn't matter if you're selling when the economy is strong or in a recession. When continually focusing on the fundamentals, evaluate your sales abilities and be aware of why and how your male customers buy from you.

Can You Sell?

Take this challenge to learn about your sales skills by answering Yes or No to the following questions:

1. Am I sociable? _____

2. Do I think in terms of success? _____

3. Do I really like selling? _____

4. Do I think of my customers' interests? _____

5. Do I read sales literature? _____

6. Do I study my prospects? _____

7. Is my personal appearance a credit to myself and the company I represent? _____

8. Do I realize that success in selling is a matter of study and perseverance, and that the element of luck is small? _____

9. Am I cheerful in the face of interruptions? _____

10. Am I always courteous even with unreasonable prospects? _____

11. Am I always scrupulously honest in my representations? _____

12. Do I think of selling as a dignified calling worthy of my best efforts? _____

13. When faced with competition, am I inspired to excel? _____

14. Do I know that my line of goods is the best on the market for its price point? _____

15. Do I try to make repeat sales? _____

16. Do I talk quality first and price later? _____

17. Do I stay with a line of goods long enough to give the line a fair trial? _____

18. Do I spend sufficient time perfecting my demonstration to make it convincing? _____

19. Do I take advantage of every modern convenience in selling? _____

20. Do I canvas systematically and never skip places because they look uninviting? _____

21. Do I work regular hours even when the weather is unpleasant? _____

22. Do I put in the extra time to close a deal
    when necessary?   _____

23. Do I put extra effort into selling after
    a poor day?   _____

24. Do I put extra effort into selling after an
    unusually good day?   _____

25. Am I determined to stick with selling despite
    the lure of easier jobs?   _____

**Score your test by adding up the number of questions
answered, "Yes." Here are your results:**

25 .... Star Saleswoman!

20 .... A Success

15 .... On the Way

Below 15..... Need Overhauling

Surprise! The above questions were published in the
December 1932 issue of *Opportunity* magazine, written for
salespeople during the Great Depression—but they're still
valid today.

Your answers to these basic questions are important to your
sales success and career. The kind of salesperson you are will
determine how you handle situations or face challenges on
a daily basis. So go back to the basics. Pick up the phone on
the first ring; follow up all contacts with a handwritten thank
you note and include your business card. Sales fundamentals
are important in the sales world. Know and apply the basics
in the sales process every time you are dealing with your
customers. If salespeople could sell through the Great
Depression, then you can certainly do it today—and it will be
much easier.

Just like the sales test, you will want your customers to say "Yes" too. It is helpful to watch body language and facial expressions, yet it's even more important to listen to their words. Your ultimate goal should be to get them to nod their head while saying Yes to buying your products and/or services. This is good news for saleswomen, not only concerning their male customers but all customers. Here's the benefit: Men speak far fewer words than women, making the word yes an easier response for men than women.

Here are five simple ways to get men to say, "Yes" on the way to closing the sale:

1. Men shy away from negativity. Throughout your sales presentation or conversations, say the word Yes more often than No. The word Yes is a positive word that helps you get them to agree with you.

2. The phrase "if we do business together" will not work for men. With a positive attitude, say, "Let's do business together." This gives them the idea that you are expecting to do business with them.

3. Be on the offense with your questions. Start by saying, "I have a question for you." This approach allows the discussion to be in your control and shows you were prepared. He most likely will answer, "Sure" or "Yes, what is it?" You have him saying Yes before getting to the ultimate question. The usual defensive question asked is, "Do you have any questions?" This puts him in an uncomfortable position, especially if he doesn't have any questions, and would most likely elicit a No response. So keep the conversation going with questions that elicit "yes" responses.

4. Never say "for the time being," "at a future date," or "at that point." Men want things to happen immediately. Instead choose words such as *now* or *today*, to get a response like, "Yes, that will work. Thank you."

5. Always believe that your potential male customer or client is ready to buy from you. Assume they *want* and *need* to talk with you. Do this even if they give you the impression it's not a good time to talk business. Be careful not to ask, "Is this a good time to talk?" To men, there is never a good time to talk. They are busy trying to make money and really don't want to chat. So, stay one step ahead of them by asking, "Is this a bad time to talk?" They most likely will say Yes. That Yes response opens the door for you to schedule a "good" time to further the discussion.

Now, you can incorporate this strategy of asking "Yes" questions throughout the sales cycle. There are phases of the sales cycle that may include discovering either the customer's perception of a product or his perception of a need that the product might satisfy. Research and evaluations are involved for both parties until the customer decides to buy.

The easiest way to remember the buying phases for males is through the "B-E-E-R Negotiation Factor." The B-E-E-R Negotiation Factor helps saleswomen understand a man's frame of mind and thought process. Besides, any negotiation, especially dealing with difficult customers, may cause you to want to drink anyway—right?

When a man drinks a beer, he usually displays his muscles by flexing them when he picks up a beer glass or bottle. This muscle flexing may reflect how he deals with his boss, spouse, friend, co-worker, or even mother-in-law. Flexing his muscles is important to him. So, to get what you want throughout a sales process, attempt to understand the following negotiation factor while making him look good—or muscular.

The B-E-E-R Negotiation Factor works like this:

B **Buildup.** First is the "getting to know you" phase. When first meeting someone or building a relationship, everyone seems to be on their best behavior. Even if you have no opportunity to go to the next phase, know that this phase is important to him. Therefore, at this point, you can ask about his family, his tie, or favorite sports team. Notice what's important to him by the information he volunteers to share with you throughout the conversation. Saleswomen need to realize it's all about "him" in this first phase.

E **Education.** In this second phase, you gather information. Your mission is to find out what problems or challenges he has, as he may be searching for answers from you. You can discover these by asking questions about his company, professional goals, or projects. For example, ask what he liked or disliked about the other companies (your competitors) that he's worked with before. Having historical data can help you know how to better service his needs in this phase. If you come across any issues that challenge you while finding solutions to his problems, share them with him. Notice how he jumps in with suggestions to fix them. This is the phase to analyze each other, so you'll most likely get a turn to share information about your company and services. Once he has an overview of your products or services, moving to the next phase brings you closer to the sale.

E **Engagement.** This is the "getting serious" phase. A difficult phase for saleswomen that could make or break a sale. You present the specific products and/or services you plan to provide. This presentation may involve commitments from him included in the contract terms, dates, and so on. Be ready to spend time presenting the answers or solutions to his problems or challenges. Earn his trust in you, your products, and/or services. Remember to continue making him feel good about his decision. Keep asking "Yes" questions to help close the sale.

R **Resolution.** This is the "morning after" phase. You've confirmed the business with a new male customer. However, the process does not stop here. Check in with him to get honest feedback assuring him that you welcome his comments. And, no matter what the outcome, let him know you appreciate his time sharing his comments. This will help you determine when or how to seek him out for future business engagements as well.

The B-E-E-R Negotiation Factor works not only for the sales process with the male consumer, but for negotiating in every facet of your life—with your spouse, kids, and even other salespeople.

Here's an interesting outlook on the B-E-E-R Negotiation factor. As mentioned, women make decisions 70 percent more slowly than men. This slows down each phase, from buildup to resolution. Janet, a hotel sales manager in New York said, "It would take 30 days or more before getting my female customers to the Engagement phase. They're waiting on their bosses to return to the office; they're visiting other competitive venues; they're still gathering information. I get frustrated just thinking about it. Whereas most of my male customers (who have the power to make the decision) prefer to go straight from the Buildup to the Resolution phase, possibly without even entering the Education and Engagement phases. Men cringe when they hear the word *engagement* anyway. They seem to want to skip that phase all together by deciding to commit or not."

Besides getting your male customer to say "Yes" throughout the B-E-E-R Negotiation Factor phases, also choose your words wisely once you reach the contract phase. Note the difference between the terms *agreement* and *contract*. You could say, "I will send you an agreement," or "Please send me a contract." Is there a difference? Sure there is! The word *agreement*, is like the word *engagement* to men. They will either not take you seriously or stop the process because most men are not comfortable with an engagement. So, instead say, "I know my services will be of value to your company, so with your approval, I'll send you the contract today." If you elicit a, "Yes," you'll know your male customer is ready to move forward with your offer. Just be careful how you use the two important words *agreement* and *contract* when in the B-E-E-R Negotiation Factor phases.

In summary, although selling to women is fine, your biggest profits will come from selling to men. You will ream more dollars faster than ever before in your sales career. Remember your sales basics and get your customer to say, "Yes" throughout the B-E-E-R Negotiation Factor phases. Then you're on your way to successful closings with your male customers.

Chapter Six

True Confessions – Male Variety

You may have heard the old saying, "I heard it straight from the horse's mouth." Well, that's just what I did—received much of my information directly through interviews with many men, who gave it to me straight indeed. In fact, I spoke with women, too. Both convinced me that they sincerely do want to conduct business with each other. When I posed curious, yet serious, questions from women to men, the answers came easier than I thought they would. In fact, throughout my interviews with men, I discovered that they wanted to share their thoughts for saleswomen but had never been asked before.

The task force I worked with carefully tallied information gathered in our interviews. So, here are the top 35 questions and answers devoted to applying knowledge (the meat and potatoes) "from the horses' mouths" in your next sales encounters with men.

Do men view good "manners" as important for saleswomen in the sales process?

Manners, in business or everyday life, are crucial to harmonious interaction between people of any gender. It's something as simply as when you recognize that you just bumped into someone or invaded his space in some way, you say, "Pardon me." It's a quick way to apologize, which demonstrates good manners. Manners indicate to others that you are civilized.

Politeness means using proper etiquette. It's a term similar to manners and a trait that men look for, especially throughout a sales process. So when your customer greets you, show your enthusiasm by smiling, extend your hand first with a firm handshake, and look your customer in the eyes.

Stand up straight and tall, and show that you're proud to have the opportunity to do business with your customer or potential customer. However, if he, himself, does not have good manners, this gives you an instant clue to question if his business is worth your time. If you're ever treated rudely by a customer with bad manners, consider how he'd treat your administrator, your staff, or anyone else in your organization after the contract is confirmed. Walk away quickly.

Are women able to create equal opportunity with men in the sales world?

They already do. Women own the sales world in companies or organizations that employ a lot of women and are looked upon as equal to men. Achieving equal opportunity takes on a greater challenge when women get into upper management positions of power, for these women become more intimidating for most men. If they are too aggressive or goal-oriented, men think, "What are they trying to prove?" If women are too timid or nonassertive in decision-making, they are considered weak. According to most men, being assertive is not bad; women can take on a helpful role for them, such as being an assistant. Yet to women, this role doesn't cut it with regard to equal opportunity.

Complaining about equal rights is not going to do any good. Whining doesn't get you anywhere either. Instead, rely on your gut feelings, experience, and knowledge. If a point or case needs to be brought up, just do it. Fight for what you believe in but do it with professionalism. Never lower your own intelligence when you know certain advice or direction is incorrect. Believe in your own voice. If not, create your own equal opportunity.

What is a man's motivation to buy?

Men don't have a motivation to buy in the way women do. Their motivation or purpose to buy mostly relates to what will make them successful or what meets their own client's goals. Men want answers to questions such as, "Does the product fill a need I have?" "Is it the best solution?" "What is the product/service like after the sale?" "Is the warranty good?" "What reputation does the company have?" From these types of questions, you can see that men focus on knowledge, problem resolution, and quality. These all precipitate from their "need," which is the most important reason for men to buy.

How can women achieve their sales objectives selling to men?

By representing their products, services, and company with integrity. A man wants a woman to be responsible for overcoming challenges from the beginning. So confront any problems or issues instead of pretending they don't exist. Mistakes happen. However, challenges and discussions about who was right or wrong waste everyone's time. If you made a mistake, say so immediately. If you don't remember how you could have caused the mistake, don't even think of apologizing. Whatever the mistake was and it's not your fault, don't allow anyone convince you otherwise. Just acknowledge you don't know the answer if you don't, but never bluff. Understand that it's okay to be wrong or questioned.

On the other hand, if you have a strong belief, don't be afraid to express your viewpoint. Just be open-minded enough to listen to others' opinions.

Like most women you may tend to be more forgiving then men when mistakes occur. Men generally aren't as forgiving as women because they don't expect themselves to make mistakes. Your reaction when mistakes occur? Stand firm on the side of right and honor. Men understand honor.

> *"I've always wondered why women seem so desperate for a sale that they need to wear a low-cut dress."*
>
> ~ Grant Holmes, Celebrity Entertainer, Canton, Ohio

Still, the "battle of the sexes" might erupt, often unfairly. During the 2008 presidential elections, when the media focused on Vice Presidential Candidate Sarah Palin's clothing expenses, she went on to donate all the clothing she wore during the campaign. Why did they not investigate her opponent Joe Biden's clothing expenses? Did he donate his clothing after the election? If it's fair for the actions of one gender to be questioned, it should be fair for the other. So be mindful about doing the right thing so both sides win. Tell your male potential customer or client why he needs to do business with you and what he can expect. His buying decision should be based on your ability to prove you deserve his trust. However, if you don't deliver on your promises, then you have only yourself to blame and not your gender.

Throughout the sales process, what is important to men?

To be trusting and respectful, and to have integrity.

Men often think, "You've got to earn my trust." However, trust is transactional, and saleswomen can use it to their advantage by *giving* trust first. The amazing thing is that when you give trust first, you have just made your customer accountable for delivering what you want—the business. When you say, "I trust you," it takes the pressure off of you and puts it on the other person to make a decision. For example, when you are in a sales situation and the relationship has been established with a male customer, tell him, "I trust that you will return my telephone call by next week," and watch his positive reaction toward you.

With trust comes respect. Men and women are different in many ways. As a saleswoman, you can learn to manage differences. However, men want to be valued first. Respect for each other is a major component of nurturing relationships. Remember, *your* success comes as a result of your customer's success. So when dealing with a man in a sales process, respect him and his position, and he will most likely treat you the same way.

The most ethical concept to abide by is integrity. When you ask, "Is integrity crucial to my sales process?" and the answer is No, you *know* you don't have integrity built in. During the sales process, it's important to know what integrity means for both you and your prospective client.

But what really is integrity? I believe integrity is about honesty—the quality of being entire or complete. It's about conducting business doing your best. The term integrity is especially used with reference to the fulfillment of contracts or promises, like keeping a meeting appointment or delivering products when scheduled. If your integrity is not intact, then your reputation can be tarnished in many ways. A person with integrity is considered to have a strong moral character— one of the most important virtues a person can possess.

If trust, respect, and integrity are so important, why don't most saleswomen learn how to apply them when working with their prospects and customers? Well, most saleswomen don't realize that it can be done. Actually, building rapport is a sales technique that can be easily accomplished by those who like to develop relationships, which refers to women in general.

Let's suppose your client is faced with an important buying decision. He wants to move 60 miles away from where he lives now to shorten his commute to work. So he needs to sell his current home and buy a new one. Whom would he entrust the sale of his most valued possession? Will he hire a charming, friendly agent with a reputation for the best marketing system, the best skills, the best negotiating ability, and the strongest affiliation with reputable real estate firm? Or will he hire one he already knows, trusts, and respects? See how important it is to posses these qualities?

Is there a difference between a man purchasing from a man versus a man purchasing from a woman?

It used to take saleswomen an average of six to seven contacts to close a sale when selling to men. However, if men are selling to men, it generally takes only two contacts to close the sale. Men believe they analyze their decisions differently when the salesperson is a woman— for no exact reason; it's just been that way for years. In today's business world, though men are softening their reluctance to buy from women because they are noticing saleswomen are more forthcoming and confident in their sales careers.

From my extensive interviews, 30 percent of men buyers said they like to deal with women in the sales process, whereas 70 percent prefer men. Generally speaking, men prefer to work with men rather than women because of their similar experiences and situations, competitive or not. They don't usually judge each other before they get to the business at hand. Remember Chapter 3 about women being their own worst enemies? Rather, men have a better comfort level that allows them to say what's on their minds when discussing business with each other. They tend to be more direct and logical than women. Also, they talk things through at their own pace and often discuss topics other than business, such as sports.

Men believe professionalism is important. They find it unprofessional and unacceptable when women get angry or cry in work situations. Emotional reactions discourage them from working with or buying from women.

Also, saleswomen usually set and work with deadlines more than male buyers do. Therefore, if women want the full benefit of selling to men, it's best to eliminate deadlines and communicate upfront that they needn't hurry with their decision. They won't feel pressured or obligated to prove anything like having to follow a deadline.

As a benefit to men, saleswomen aren't likely to be as combative or competitive as salesmen. It's probably because women learned to "play nice" with dolls, playing house, and playing school. Men were raised rambunctiously, playing with toy trucks and in sports. Because men and women have had different ways of playing (and therefore conducting business), men regard women as no "real" competition.

Bill Morton, a hospitality sales manager, said, "If I buy a big-ticket item such as a car or high-end electronic product, it's a male bonding moment to talk technical with another man who clearly would understand my needs. If I'm buying clothes, I prefer a saleswoman so I can get opinions on what looks good or not. If I am buying a home, I would prefer a female agent. She sees 'practical' concerns whereas I would only see space for my flat screen and BBQ grill."

There are times men drag out the sales process when working with women, mainly because they enjoy having women pay attention to them. Consequently, men tend to spend more time shopping with a saleswoman than a salesman. If this happens, he may just be enjoying the business relationship. However, the decision process still generally goes more quickly for selling to men than selling to women consumers.

How can you tell if a man wants to dominate the sales process?

Plain and simple, consider his EGO!

That means a man usually wants to be known as the decision maker, the one in control. Look for signs. Does he open a door for you and greet you like a guest? Does he play host or simply wave you into his office? Does he scurry behind his desk or pull up a chair for you at the conference table?

Be aware of his possible desire to dominate. When greeted or approached, always remain standing up and look him in the eye. If you do decide to sit down, never sit on the other side of his desk facing him. The only time you should sit down is when "equal and separate" chairs are available. The sitting arrangement should allow a mutual, face-to-face, open exchange of conversation without any obstructions (like a desk) in the way.

Do give your customer an opportunity to share with you as much information as possible. This encourages him to feel comfortable and confident in your presence.

"Many of the best sales professionals I know are women. They need to rely on their knowledge, talents, and skills and by creating a professional image through how they dress, inspire long-term success in the business relationships they manage."

~ Bruce M. MacMillan - President & CEO - Meeting Professionals International, Dallas, Texas

The more confident the man is, the less need he'll have to dominate the situation. David Wheat with Axiom

---

Advisors, LLC *(www.axiom123.com)* explained it this way: "Selling tools to customers at Home Depot is quite different than selling services to the CEO of Home Depot. The situation is also defined by the scope of the buying decision. Egos could easily play a part depending on the superior that the saleswomen will be dealing with. Saleswomen will need to determine if the sale affects only the buyer, or if it also affects the company itself. Usually, the ego will stand out enough in order to know how to handle the situation. Be aware of it, but stick to your sales process without stroking or breaking down their egos. Encountering a customer with an ego is delicate, so stick with the facts and always tell the truth about what they need."

A skillful professional goes *through* the buyer's ego to persuade and convince. There's an old saying, "Men won't stop and ask for directions." If Christopher Columbus didn't need directions, then neither do they! Ego takes full rein here; men don't want to be told what to do or how to get to their destination. Besides, according to most men, asking for help shows weakness. The answer? Provide a map or directions immediately in your conversations, e-mail messages, and any other communications. These can successfully bypass the male ego.

Timing is important, too. Help him by acknowledging his busy schedule with a statement such as, "I understand this is not a good time. May I contact you tomorrow to further discuss our services for your company?" No matter what the outcome, he'll appreciate this approach and most likely will see you the next time without his ego taking a prominent role.

When selling to men, are details important?

Generally, men don't want to worry about any details. When a couple is planning to get married, who takes care of the details? It's not the man!

Women, on the other hand, enjoy spending *months* on wedding details to make the day perfect. Not that the men don't want the same perfection; they're just busy doing other things. The bride coordinates the wedding date, flowers, church location, guests and bridesmaids, the cake, the written vows, and hundreds of other details to create a memorable event. The groom, on the other hand, picks up his tux the day before the wedding and asks what time he should arrive. Some men don't even want to know *that* much.

Men usually feel the same way about details in a sales process. They prefer not to be the one to work them out; they have other fish to fry. What does this tendency tell saleswomen? *They* have to implement the details—graphics, charts, facts and figures—working them out internally so the men don't have to deal with them.

Ironically, men tend to gravitate toward detailed statistics more than women. This means if you discuss details in your sales presentation or in any conversation with men, be direct, logical, concise, and to the point. Men expeditiously benefit from all your preparation of the details. If the details need to be discussed, take your time presenting them, realizing that the male buyer hasn't spent time with the information like you have. Some people, men included, may be more detailed-oriented and analytical than others, and may ask probing questions. So, once again, saleswomen must have the facts and figures on hand to back up their presentations in case they're requested. However, details can be overwhelming to men when presented all at once. So, chose wisely how you present your products, services and you.

What are the best reasons for men to purchase products or services from women?

The previous answer stated that statistics, graphs, and facts are great ways to present to men. The following table is an example of just that. It displays the results of a survey of 430 men from many different industries and professions. On a scale of 1 to 5, with 5 being the most important, the chart below clearly indicates the level of importance men attach to characteristics when buying from saleswomen.

How 430 Men Rated Characteristics of Saleswomen in the Buying Process

Characteristics	Most Important 5	4	3	Least Important 2	1
Personality	6.0%	36.4%	9.1%	45.5%	3.0%
Knowledge of Product/Service	76.6%	15.2%	4.2%	4.0%	0.0%
Sales Skill	9.1%	30.3%	51.5%	6.1%	3.0%
Low-Cut Dress	6.1%	2.5%	16.1%	34.0%	41.3%
Trust	21.1%	56.5%	18.1%	1.1%	3.2%

From the five characteristics of saleswomen (listed from most important to least important), knowledge of product/service is the number one reason (76.6%) men buy from women. Trust (56.5%) is the next most important characteristic for saleswomen, followed by Sales Skill (51.5%) and Personality (45.5%). Notice that wearing a Low-Cut Dress (41.3%) is considered the least important by these 430 men. Therefore, according to this survey, if saleswomen have knowledge of their product or service, trust, good sales skills, and a pleasant personality (no anger or crying!), men are more likely to purchase a product or service from them.

How should saleswomen negotiate with men?

Few men "see" a gender difference when it comes to negotiations. Most men take their feelings out of the equation when negotiating by sticking with the facts. If the saleswoman provides good service with straight, clear answers to questions, she most likely will win the sale.

Men want to be right, so avoid doing anything to make them feel foolish or unintelligent. You risk losing both the business and the potential relationship. Instead, use partnership statements like these: "John, you're right, and since you know that, let's do this . . . " Then be prepared to apply your best negotiation techniques when it's time to close the sale.

To negotiate well, be careful not to give away everything. Your customer will not respect you and neither will your boss, who might reprimand you for doing so. Give your customer the facts to make the decision, but not a lot of fluff. Tell him you know he's busy and you respect his time. He should be looking at your proposal or listening to your presentation with interest. Men want a good negotiation process, not distractions. Bring to the table all of your ammunition to "wow" him. If he recognizes that you have good negotiation skills, it won't matter that you're a woman. If he is married, appropriately include his wife in your comments. Don't forget to use the B-E-E-R Negotiation Factor, too. If he requests alone time with you, then he is not interested in your business.

How does a saleswoman find out what is important to their male customers?

Asking direct questions specific to the purchase allows you to learn what is important to your customers, including their interests and/or concerns. Use a category approach—major, middle, or minor.

A "major" category consists of items or issues that not only have high priority for your male customer, but hold little room to negotiate. For example, he may have to adhere to a certain budget to buy your telecommunications product. Take this need seriously because he will take his business elsewhere if you challenge him on it.

The second, or "middle," category allows more flexibility to maneuver within his requirements than those in the "major" category. Although still important, they're not deal-breakers for him. For example, his budget to purchase your product may be available, but only if you can prove the product or service will solve a problem for him the long term.

The third category is of "minor" importance to him— and perhaps be of more value to you, as the salesperson or your company. Let's say your customer wants your product or service but needs only one month's order at a time due to the lack of his office storage space.

Therefore, he decides to buy from you but signs a contract that commits him to your product or service one month at a time. This is a winning combination for both parties in a sales process because the customer receives the product on a "need" bases and the salesperson gets the business.

To meet his objectives—and yours—ask questions in all three categories. Find out what's important and then you can tailor your product or service to meet his requirements.

How do men decide when making a purchase?

Once they know all the information and details, most male consumers adopt a "now or never" mindset that gives them a strong reason to make a decision. Remember, men make decisions that will help them make more money or solve a problem; women make decisions to intrinsically enhance their lives.

If you're encountering a particular male consumer for the first time, ask other salespeople who know him to answer this question for him (or ask him directly): "What is the best buying decision you ever made? How did you make your decision?" Men expect they will have a beneficial exchange when the salesperson understands their buying needs.

Once your male customer decides to buy, be prepared to provide what you promise. If he's not ready to purchase, you need to back off and tell him how much you appreciated his attention during the process. If you use this approach, he will likely contact you when he's ready to buy.

How long does it take for men to make a purchase decision?

That depends on the scope of the decision. No matter what the process, expect it to go fairly quickly if the man is immediately interested. It's important, though, to find out if the decision directly affects him, the company, or his family. If a man is buying a big-screen TV for his home, for example, he will use a different decision-making process than if he is purchasing software for his business. Purchasing a TV may be more of an emotional decision due to his personal interest and his family's involvement. His decision to purchase software could be based on several factors, from the company's budget to how many people will be using it.

"In business ... women are men in sheep's clothing ..."

~ Martin Franklin, Chairman & CEO, Jargen Corporation, New York

To get an idea of how long the purchase process will take, ask your prospective buyer about the importance of his choice. Is there a lot riding on it? Find out if he is the sole decision-maker or whether the final decision will be made by a committee or his boss. Typically, a man's personal decision will take longer than a business decision because of the emotion involved.

Consider your own sales deadline. If one prospect takes too long to meet your deadline, move on to another prospect and come back when he's ready to buy. However, be aware that men like to keep their options open in case they change their minds or become ready to purchase in the future. So be sure you're prepared when they're ready to buy.

What is the best way for saleswomen to offer solutions to male buyers?

Men want options. If you can't meet their needs with your products or services, suggest other solutions! Maybe you will even have to research your competitors to make sure they get what they want. Or, maybe you will just have to "MOON" your customer. No, this is not what you may think! Moon, a technique called Multiple Offers Of Negotiations™, it works well in the sales world. As a matter of fact, salespeople can be quite good at "MOONing" their customer's, and the best part is they don't even realize they're doing it.

Here's how it works. You have already built your relationship with your potential customer, and he is ready to buy your services. You receive his requests, or wish list, which can be one long list in no particular order. This can be overwhelming and confusing to a saleswoman. From the list, you have to guess what's really important to your customer. As the saleswoman, you want to do the best possible so you can earn his business. So, you write "Ok" or "Yes" next to the items you are able to approve and for the non-approved items, you provide alternatives.

Here is a MOON example: Suppose your male customer asks for nine suite upgrades at a hotel for his meeting but you have only ten suites available altogether during his preferred dates. So you compromise and give him six suites. Then you review the "No" items checked on the list to determine what you can offer in place of the requested items. A "No" item could be that your customer asked for a complimentary cocktail reception for 200, but your hotel isn't budgeted for it. Therefore, the "No" item couldn't be approved and you risk losing the business because of it. So, you MOON your customer by offering something else that's not on his list. Yep—that's right, you offer a new option altogether. It may be something that your company had provided other clients in the past and it worked well. So, instead of a complimentary reception, you might offer a tray of beverages in the lobby during the group arrival time. Remember, though, this is a case-by-case situation.

The point is this: Your male customer will know you're trying your best to meet his needs if you MOON him with something new. It allows an opening for both parties to move the sales process forward and come closer to sealing the deal.

Do women need to know about the sports world to converse with men?

For the majority of men I interviewed, this question had an easy answer—Yes!

The wonderful world of sports is a great topic to start or end a conversation, depending on whether the saleswoman can target the sports team or event her customer is interested in. Sports talk can be effective even during a break in the sales process. If women want to participate in this kind of discussion with men, they need to understand the competitive arena in which men live, love, learn, and play, and they need to show genuine interest. Otherwise men might be insulted or negatively judge a woman who uses this strategy ineptly. Think about if the roles were reversed by having a salesman talking to you about your makeup. He would have to know about the ingredients, the brands and competitors, applications, and to talk with you about the cosmetic industry. If the man is not already in the cosmetic industry, this would require a lot of homework and research to talk with you about it. Therefore, approach this topic carefully, appropriately, and sincerely. Otherwise, it might backfire.

Your best move is to make sports talk fun by having a favorite team or player of your own. Men enjoy challenges when it comes to sports trivia, too. A woman can score high by knowing team names, mascots, or rules. The same strategy may be used with music, TV shows, or any other male interests. Judy Ashcroft, an assistant for Bank of America, was listening to her customer and discovered he enjoys the popular TV show, *CSI*. She started watching the show and can now relate to him better in their conversations. It's an easy process—and it works!

So sit back and watch his favorite show or a sports channel and take advantage of this easy sales strategy.

What impresses male buyers about saleswomen?

Professionalism and finding common ground with men. Knowing something about sports, the stock market or learning about their families, will help you build rapport. Men look for creativity, too. Anything that sparks their interest will differentiate you and help win the sale.

Generally, men won't turn down a sales appointment with a woman because, ultimately, they enjoy women's company. Their motives may be only to casually connect with women, so keep this in mind—an appointment doesn't automatically mean a sale.

What is the best way for a woman to be professional? Be on time, be natural, do what you say you will do, finish what you start, and thank your customer for the business. These may sound like simple steps, but they're important, and men know if a woman neglects them. On the other side of the coin, the professional saleswoman must develop effective radar for men who waste her time.

What is the MOST important skill a saleswoman needs?

It's all about *what you know*, which can be learned. Sometimes, saleswomen have a difficult time understanding the value of doing research to learn about their customers or their customers' business. Having this knowledge, however, is so powerful that it inspires confidence, translates into added value, and can drive the customer's decision-making. Not only must saleswomen know about their customers' needs, but they must know their own products and services very well.

If you have little or no knowledge about your product or service, without hesitation, men will not buy from you, nor will they provide you with any future opportunities to present to them. In the end, your lack of knowledge will drive them to your competitors, and the trust factor disappears. They will not refer you to others, either. If you are average in your knowledge, men may make a moderate investment in time and money, and then not buy from you again unless you prove your promises or performance. Also, they may say critical things to other men about you, but most likely behind your back.

But if you become knowledgeable about your business, products, and/or services and are professional in your presentation, men will make the time and money investments, while building a strong and continuous business relationship with you. They will even compliment you in front of others. When this happens, you know you're on good terms. Continue servicing these customers, provide strategies and resources, and earn referrals, too.

Actions do indeed speak louder than words.

How should women prepare to sell to men?

Positive self-talk can help you prepare for a sales presentation, appointment, or meeting. Get yourself (and only you) in a huddle and cheer yourself on before the big day. Let your energy level and tone of voice rise. Eat right, exercise, and get a good night's sleep prior to "game day." Arrive early, visit the restroom and visualize your presentation, look in the mirror with a big smile on your face, and give yourself credit for taking on this mission. You want to display that "pumped up" first-impression attitude when you walk into your customer's office.

Men have a way of testing a saleswoman to make sure they're dealing with a professional. So have a good sense of humor, concentrate on your customer's questions, and give the right answers to the best of your ability. Most importantly, do your homework and make all the right moves to put your strategy into play. Think about it: in football, if the quarterback (in this case, you) doesn't know the plays, would the other players (your customers) know what to do?

How do women sell to men— soft sell or hard sell?

There are many ways to sell to men. The men who were

interviewed especially wanted to make clear they're only interested in a soft-sell approach. The less pressure saleswomen put on men, the easier they'll be able to close the sale. In fact, any type of aggressive hard sell makes men completely uncomfortable.

Men make purchases based on need and/or perceived need. For example, say your in the retail industry and your customer tries on a business suit. As a saleswoman, you compliment him on how nice the jacket looks and how well the slacks fit. A man may not even need the business suit but because you affirmed the positive way he looks, he buys it. Women are known to be more intuitive than men, so use your intuition to create the perception of a need and you will make the sale.

In addition, many women miss the opportunity to ask for the business. Instead, they hope men will jump in the air like Michael Jordan after hearing the presentation and shout, "YES! I'll buy from you today!"

The reality is, men want to be "needed" throughout the entire sales process. So you have to repeat, "I'd like to earn your business" at intervals throughout the process. Of course, provide answers first, then go for the close by asking for their business. Once you pose the question, shut up and listen to him.

Selling to men is also influenced by how you engage them throughout the process. Because men like to "fix" things you can help them help you close the sale when you sense they really want to buy. Back to the retail profession example, offer several belts to go with the slacks. Let him know that all the belts would work great but suggest one you know he would prefer. Once he chooses the belt he likes, compliment him again on his excellent choice. However, be honest with his selections too. After all, you want others to ask him where he bought such a great business suit. This strategy works all the time.

In some situations, it's highly advantageous for a company to have female sales representatives. In cosmetics, for example, men don't understand the fundamentals of cosmetic products and applications. Therefore, women have the upper hand when selling lipstick or perfume to men to give their wives or girlfriends. Know how to advertise or market to attract men to your product or services will solve their problems. Selling to men in their unknown territory such as cosmetics allows your expertise to shine immediately.

Is it true that men don't know what they want when purchasing a product?

It's not that men don't know what they want; they just have no opinion nor do they really care what product line or service they buy *if it exactly meets their needs.*

Typically, a purchase for a man is a logical one and rarely an emotional one. A logical purchase is a "now" purchase—sometimes no matter what the price or how you deliver it, as long as it will better him or his company. It may be furniture for his new office. In his mind, he knows actually what he wants and is not concerned with anyone's suggestions, so leave the price quote and delivery details for last in your presentations.

Sometimes, men will make an emotional purchase just to impress a woman. When he does, he most likely will ask the opinion of a saleswoman, his sister, or his mother before purchasing. It's like what Bill Morton said earlier; he would prefer working with saleswomen when he buys clothes so he can get opinions on what looks good or not. If he is buying a new home, another fairly emotional purchase, he would prefer a woman agent. Both situations show that men have specific goals, and they know how to get support, if needed, for their purchases. Remember, however, that men need good reasoning, statistics, data, or facts to support their decisions to buy products that will meet their needs and goals.

What is the one thing saleswomen should NOT do when selling to men?

NEVER humiliate them. Nothing is more important to a man than his own reputation. If you're making a businessman look insecure, incapable, or incompetent, he will always remember you for it—and not fondly. Whether you get him to disclose a bad golf score or admit to losing a client or account to a competitor—or even tell him you saw him lose a fight for a parking spot—you put him on the defense.

On a more upbeat note, giving compliments show thoughtfulness, whether business-related or not. Flatter him on his golf swing, the color of his car, or how well he did with the presentation to his new clients.

Do men regard price being important to the purchasing process?

If you want to receive big bucks from men buying from you, then take this question seriously. Men believe they are more logical than price conscious. Most will lean toward high-priced items but they don't rely on price for their ultimate decision. And you can be sure they focus on the quality of the product or service. Most men want and focus on value before price! This is completely the opposite from women consumers.

Economists say that "value" is a term indicating "satisfaction is raised from a good." That means a man will pay $2 for a $1 product he needs or values, whereas a woman will pay $1 for a $2 product that she doesn't necessarily value or need, just because it's on sale. If "value" is proven, men willingly pay for it. This is a strong reason why men constitute a largely untapped consumer market that will bring huge dollars into your pocketbook. So find out what your product/services offer *above and beyond the price.*

How do successful saleswomen handle the "Good Old Boys" club?

You've heard the saying, "If you can't beat 'em, join 'em." In the sales world, however, if women decide on this tactic, it could be disadvantageous to their sales.

The "Good Old Boys" network started back in the early 20th century as fraternal groups met to share ideas about business. As more women entered the business world, these groups or clubs actually grew stronger. Men deny that it had anything to do with being insecure, saying men just wanted to hang onto their close connections among their own gender.

The best way to handle a Good Old Boys Club is to stay away from the group and target one member at a time. Find at least one member who is approachable and become his friend. Get him to help you move into contact with the rest of the group. For the most powerful effect, don't stay long when you do get into the group. This idea may be difficult to grasp, but you don't want the group to think you're trying to take over. So you need to step in and out like a dance on stage so you're not perceived as overstepping their boundaries. Before you know it, they will remember to call you when they have business needs.

Make sure you graciously thank the friend who made it possible for you to accomplish this feat when you do.

What simple advice should women take in throughout the sales process?

Be approachable. Read verbal and nonverbal communication cues. Extend a firm handshake and smile. Of course, as mentioned before, know your product/services along with your strengths and weaknesses. Don't shy away from your weaknesses; men *want* to see you as another human, but also show confidence. It's about being "natural." Women trying too hard (by wearing a low-cut dress) head for failure. But women who are fun and friendly see the truth about how to sell to men.

Most importantly, men don't like to be sold to; they'd rather be supported with pertinent information and educated on specifics. Do that by grabbing their attention with questions. For example, because of today's electronic communication devices, questions and answers are short and direct. However, if you ask open-ended questions starting with "how" and "why," you'll likely receive more information. Asking the right questions is powerful. But, more than that listen to the answers. Don't think about what to say next—just listen. Hear him state his needs first, and then offer him answers.

Most men have women assistants. How do women get past these gatekeepers?

Go personal: Call your customer's administrator or assistant, male or female, from time to time to get to know him or her. Become friends and ask questions about how the person works with the boss. Work with the assistant, too. Follow up with any requests and be sincere. Send a card or a small gift to him or her, or something personal for the kids with complimentary messages. However, be careful of your agenda with this strategy. You want to remember what you're trying to accomplish and stick with your purpose. Gatekeepers could get caught up in your kindness and attention.

You may find that voicemail is the only gatekeeper, which will give you access to the decision maker, if only indirectly at first. Try calling early, at noon, or in the evening, as you never know when the boss may pick up his phone. Most likely, though, you will reach his voicemail. How you leave your message will determine how quickly—or *if*—he will return your call.

In a friendly voice, give clear instructions on what you would like him to do. For example, to have him return your call, speak slowly when providing your phone number. As the receiver on the other end, you know how frustrating it can be if you have to listen to a message over and over just to catch the phone number. It's important to be concise and talk in a natural tone of voice. Don't talk through the entire voicemail time by laying down all the information. Instead, give him just enough to entice him to call back wanting more information from you. If you aren't sure of your customer's demeanor or have never talked to him before, call his voicemail to hear his tone and attitude. Does he seem friendly? Professional? Boring? Bossy? Use what you find out to strategize how to approach him in future conversations.

How should women handle the "short man syndrome" in a sales process?

Many men have the short man syndrome, which is known as lacking confidence due to their height. That certainly doesn't mean they don't make wise decisions— nor does it mean you owe them something because of their complex. If you deal with a male customer who has this hang-up, play to his ego a bit to help him get past that ridiculous fixation. Find other qualities you can compliment him on. Treat him like any of your other customers. It might be helpful to remember the saying, "A real man can look up to a woman."

How should saleswomen deal with men who operate in the "fix-it" mode?

In general, men think they are an information center. They like to know everything from stocks and sports to world news and more. Since they were little boys, they were programmed to fix things, from broken toys to the wheels on their skateboards to the handlebars on their bicycles. Men enjoy fixing things to prove their worth, overcome challenges, and figure things out before asking for help. Men are into the "figuring it out" mode much earlier than women.

In the business world, this fix-it tendency rears its head in the sales process quite often. When women talk about a situation without answers, men assume they're looking for a repair, a fix, or suggestions.

Grant Holmes, CCO for AkivaTech, a marketing and web-branding company from Canton, Ohio, shared his insight: "When I work with female clients, I often ask lots of questions. I have to decide, am I listening so they can talk through something or listening to gather clues to help fix the issue? It's true that it is men's nature to want to fix things, just as it is women's nature to want to 'talk about things.' When men are in a fix-it mode, you can either let us fix it or ask if we can just talk about the situation instead. For women who do not want something fixed, I recommend they start the conversation with, 'I need to talk through something and I need clarity, but I'm not looking for you to fix this. Can we do that?' This type of statement would make men's lives (in general) so much easier."

"Considering that most women understand the power of their own generation, they also have the power to choose wisely on who they are and what they wear."

~ Phil Goodman, President & CEO of Genergraphics, Inc., San Diego, California

Grant went on to say, "If a woman does not want suggestions or something fixed, I thank her for the advice and tell her I will consider it. If a woman decides to ask for help in resolutions or situations, letting the man 'fix things' will get her on his good side. After all, sales is a game."

What's the best strategy to win over difficult male customers?

Difficult male customers can be frustrating for saleswomen. There can be many reasons a particular customer isn't cooperating the way you want him to. He may be demanding, complicated, unmanageable or just plain stubborn. Maybe he's having a bad work day and you just happen to be the one he vents to at that time. Or maybe he's just not interested in hearing your presentation. If you run across a difficult customer and are convinced he needs to know about your products or service, then it's best to partner with a male co-worker or boss as a buffer.

"Team selling" changes the dynamics of the sale process. The team selling approach incorporates a second point of view that helps the decision-making process get solidified. When you team sell with the right partner, you typically have a greater chance to receive the business.

Overall, the sales process is easier when using a team effort to close the sale with men. Plus, you create a relationship on a new level that is comfortable to men, who like to have several people helping them. It makes them feel special and well taken care of throughout the sales process. However, be aware that once you introduce your new team member to your prospects, it is often hard to go it alone once the customer has been exposed to the team experience.

At times, your new team member and a potential customer may become quite friendly through their male bonding experience. When this happens, the customer might venture to ask questions on the side like "Is she single?" or "Do you think she'd like to meet me in the bar to discuss the deal?" Make sure your partner shuts down these comments immediately by sticking with the facts and the purpose of the relationship. So don't choose a partner just to have a partner.

If team selling is not available for you, make sure you maximize your skills that include sales fundamentals. Be prepared for comments like "It must be easy to sell looking as good as you do." Just ignore such comments and quickly respond by speaking in the lower range of your voice with confidence. Say, "Thank you; however, do you see our products and services assisting you at this time?" Avoid any giggling; just stay relaxed and in control, and always smile. Write notes throughout the conversation to show you're seriously interested in what your customer is saying.

What is the best way for saleswomen to learn about the customer and his company?

In general, salespeople tend to experience intimidation because of the pressure or fear of rejection. A lack of knowledge can cause those anxieties which can be detrimental. However, gaining knowledge of the customer or company becomes a matter of doing the research and asking questions. Knowledge and confidence diminish or eliminate fear that may be felt before gathering the information needed.

No saleswoman should try to shortcut the process with, "Here are the features and benefits—want to buy?" Applying a hard sell won't gain the respect you want from your male customer, and he certainly won't buy from you. Before you meet, research his company thoroughly. Ask appropriate questions before you present your products and/or services. Learn all his needs as if you have only one chance to make the sale.

How you present your products or services will depend on what you have learned about your customer and his company. EVERYTHING is important to men—features, benefits, warranty, costs, company reputation, and more.

How can women gain possession of "the remote control" in the sales process?

According to a majority of men interviewed, taking the remote control away when they're watching TV is like depriving them of air. Such an act seriously infringes on their personal domain, because having that control allows men time to think and take in only the information that's important to them. Lots of women believe the remote control is a physical version of a man's alter ego.

Men hate commercials. They switch channels until they find something that interests them, and commercials just don't pass the test. Case in point: One commercial shows a woman wearing a low-cut dress either washing a car or seductively drinking a beer. Men will watch about half the commercial, if that, then keep switching channels until they end up back at the same show they were watching in the first place. Even the "low-cut dress" commercials are short-lived when men have the remote control.

How does a man's remote control behavior relate to sales? It relates to how they conduct business. When they're interested in a product or service, they become stimulated by the idea of having it. Remember, some men are impulsive buyers, but if they're not completely excited about the product and/or service, they need time to think about it, digest it, or sit with it before making a decision. Therefore, the more complex the presentation, the longer it takes them to take action or make a decision.

Having the "remote control" allows men to sit down, think and stop the action whenever they want. Sometimes they don't even watch TV to watch TV; they are likely to use this time to relax while making a decision in their heads on a matter or figuring out their next steps in a particular situation.

So who really gets possession of the remote control? Well, at home, a woman can politely ask for it and let her man know she wants to watch a cooking channel to learn how to make a great dinner for him. Or she can let him know she will compromise by flipping the channels when the commercials come on so he remains interested. Or how about suggesting your man go on a weekend fishing trip with the guys so you can hold the remote control for a few days. And guess what? Similar strategies work in sales, too.

How does a saleswoman discover a man's communication style?

The style of men's communication may be direct, confrontational, quite, analytical, dominate, rude, straightforward, thoughtful, strategic and many other ways. However, this style may be taken out of context. For example, sometimes saleswomen encounter foul language or rude comments, which can be quite uncomfortable in a sales process. A man might say, "Look at that. She's wearing a business suit like a man." Most likely, he's not saying she's unprofessional; he's just commenting, and he's obviously comfortable enough to speak his mind to you. The best way for the saleswoman to handle a communication style like this is not to analyze what he said but to draw him back to the subject discussion within the sales process at hand.

How can a saleswoman discretely give men instructions during the sales process?

As previously mentioned, men don't like to ask for directions. Nor do they like to *take* directions. Again, it's a matter of ego. However, men appreciate directions or instructions if they are given in the right way. Consider that a best-selling gadget for men is the GPS used when driving. If a man has this system, he is actually "asking" for directions—but receiving them from a new-fangled gadget, which is just fine.

Men need and want directions and instructions, but they don't like to ask for them, nor do they like being told what to do. Therefore, it's wise when selling to a man to provide "suggestions," or explain instructions from the perspective of "this is the way it works," not "do it this way." You could also give him written instructions that are standard with your product or service and sufficiently explain what they say. That way he won't have to ask and won't think you're telling him what to do. He most likely will wait and read it while sitting on the toilet anyway. Overall, he will appreciate having the information and thank you for relating it in a professional manner.

What do men admire about professional saleswomen?

Men admire saleswomen who are real, genuine. They want women to be themselves. They especially admire saleswomen who are knowledgeable about conducting their business and do their homework so no one's time is wasted. Men can tell if a saleswoman understands and conducts an effective sales process from the introduction to the follow-up, and they appreciate women who strive to gain insights about their male customers during this process. In short, men admire saleswomen who can present the whole package without the heels high and the low blouse.

So how do men feel about the way women dress?

Even though most men enjoy the "low-cut dress" way of dressing, 97 percent of the men interviewed are uncomfortable with it in a business setting. Surprisingly, men don't understand why women flaunt their bodies and don't leave anything for the imagination. Remember Chapter 1? Mark experienced similar concerns for his co-worker Rhonda's "low-cut dress" sales strategy. Men said they'd honestly prefer to see women succeed than wear a "low-cut dress" in the business world.

Is it wise to have sex with your male customer to close a sale?

NO! You risk it costing you, your reputation, your job, your sales, your future, your life—PERIOD! Notice how short the answer is to this question.

Sales Buster Moves

Chapter Seven

10 Strategies on How To Sell to Men

The previous chapter presented valuable information from hundreds of men who willingly shared how they would prefer saleswomen to deal with them throughout a sales process. How does it feel to gain insights into a man's way of thinking?

This chapter offers 10 strategies based on those insights that you can use to enhance your abilities to sell to a man. It doesn't matter if you're selling him a tie, convincing him to give you a raise at work, or wanting him to take out the garbage—it's all selling! Use these 10 strategies to be successful.

1. **Understand your competition and know your competitive type.**

   Have you ever heard Chris Berman on ESPN say, *"Go all the way!"?* Well, that's what men do when it comes to competition. Competitive by nature, their ultimate goal is to WIN. Women don't think about "winning" as much as men do, yet they still need to understand the game of competition—and men expect them to. After all, competition plays a big part in being successful in society.

From the moment people wake up until they go to sleep at night, they're competing in some way or another.

From changing lanes in traffic to rushing to get into the shortest airport security line or fastest checkout line at the grocery store, people compete. There isn't one person, male or female, who hasn't experienced this, and there's no situation that can't be regarded as competition. Yes, you might hear "let's have a win/win situation." Yet when you give up something or compromise in your negotiations, this relays the message that winning isn't all that important. Overall, if you really want something, the best competitive frame of mind is to go for the win, just like men do. So get tough by pursuing what you want in any situation. Use your skills, knowledge, and persistence to state your case on why you want to win.

Winning is fun and having fun is winning. Winning boosts self-esteem, builds confidence, and creates an opportunity to celebrate. Yet, if you don't "win," you "lose," and no one wants to be in that situation because losing is considered bad, stressful, depressing, and disappointing. I believe the only thing we don't mind losing is our excess weight!

People respond to competition in different ways depending on their competitive type—and it's a good idea to know your own type. To explain this, let me lighten this up a bit by giving an example that men and women can both relate to. It features their "best friend" the dog.

A great love of my life is my 1 year old dog, Chief. If you have a dog or animal you care for, you know how you see life through your pet—especially if things happen like they go after your shoes which Chief does from time to time. I get to practice my unconventional love for him because I really like my shoes.

One day I went to the dog park with Chief. I wanted to get a sense of what dogs do when they're around each other and to observe similarities between dogs and humans. As I watched all the different types of dogs within the area, it amazed me how they were drawn to each other, sniffing, playing, and checking each other out. Their various behaviors helped me delineate a few competitive types I also observe in human beings.

———⋙◦⋘———

The first competitive type I identified was the *aggressive* type. Everyone has seen a mean-looking dog who growls, snaps, and steals from other dogs. Such dogs have a bully mentality. They lash out in overly competitive ways. It seems they'll do anything to win or get one-up on others. The saying "it's a dog-eat-dog world" refers to this type of mentality. You can see it when a saleswoman rushes through her presentation to go straight for the kill. Her closing question might be a pushy, "Are you ready to sign on the dotted line?" as she shoves the contract under the customer's nose. This aggressive type "bares her teeth" and dares to pull any stunt to win. In the end, a "dog attack" could turn on her and rip her apart.

Barbara, a buyer for a retail store in Minneapolis, experienced being "bitten in the backside" for being too aggressive and greedy. She had been servicing a particular customer for five years, and his account came up for renewal, so she prepared another contract. But this year, Barbara increased his pricing and even took away some critical concessions that her client, Mr. Thomas, had always received on an annual basis. Confident Mr. Thomas would sign the contract anyway, she mailed it with a short letter of instructions instead of hand-delivering it as in previous years.

This concerned Mr. Thomas because he'd had some difficulties with one of Barbara's departments and wanted to discuss the situation face to face. So when Mr. Thomas received the contract by mail, he set it aside, deciding to take his time by searching for an alternative company.

A few weeks later, Barbara called asking for the contract and was told by an assistant that another company had been selected. How do you think Barbara reacted when she heard this news? Probably shocked, devastated, and disbelieving that she just lost one of her most profitable accounts. She left a message for her client, Mr. Thomas, to ask him what happened. It was too late; he had firmly made up his mind.

In hindsight, Barbara certainly took advantage of the business and the relationship, and missed an important opportunity at her client's contract renewal time. She'd learned that she should have checked in throughout the year to make sure her company's services were running smoothly for Mr. Thomas, meeting him face to face and delivering the contract to his office. She could have captured the concern he had with one of the departments, discussed it, and took time to solve the problem. But instead, Barbara's aggressive and greedy style aced her and her company out of a long-time loyal client.

———»·•·«———

Or are you the **submissive** type? You may have seen the kind of dog who gives in to other dogs, rolls over, or plays dead. Similarly, women respond submissively when they don't have confidence in their own value. They habitually defer to their spouses, kids, bosses, and customers. This competitive type is actually not competitive *enough*; they give up control and sabotage their own actions, thus sabotaging themselves. Self-sabotage typically results from being a submissive type, and it can send women into a tailspin of depression if not recognized.

One of the most difficult areas for saleswomen to deal with is the sales presentation. This stems from being in a situation of self promotion. If a saleswoman can't confidently promote herself and her ideas, products, and/or services, making a presentation can be difficult.

To many women, self-promotion is "a guy thing." Men find it easy to sell themselves to get ahead in life. Women in general don't want to get ahead in this way; they want to work hard, be considered good at what they do, and be recognized for it.

———»·•·«———

Cindy, who owns a small publishing company, was preparing for a presentation to a large company to receive their employee manual business. Cindy was so excited about the opportunity, she could only see dollar signs flashing in front of her eyes. But even though she could visualize the end result, she missed the opportunity to ask the right questions and conduct her research properly. She became more obsessed with what she'd wear to the presentation than the business at hand. Consequently, her presentation went off track and she didn't clearly promote herself and the solutions her client wanted to hear.

In Cindy's case, self-sabotage came into play. That's why it's important to take yourself seriously when self-promotion is required. You want to tap into your feelings of confidence—the quality saleswomen need most! You gain confidence by becoming comfortable promoting yourself and your strengths, and throwing away any submissive tendencies.

So do your research and ask the right questions before any presentation, and always before counting the dollars you haven't earned yet. The results will come if you work the journey of self-promoting.

———

The ideal—the *wise* competitive type is the most successful way to win. This is the type of dog everyone gravitates toward. They are happy, smart, well-behaved, friendly, and likeable to play with. This salesperson's traits include a calming manner and being personable, intelligent, in control, loving, and confident. She believes in collaboration—a winning response to competition!

When saleswomen realize that type is not about the other person but about them as individuals, they can become more accountable for their actions. The wise type respects others and helps them solve problems. Though not always easy, being wise means taking the winning path that includes gathering advice as well as listening to their intuition, experiences, and knowledge. Ultimately, the wise type makes the right choices to benefit the most people.

Obviously in the earlier example, Barbara didn't practice wisdom in her decisions. She not only neglected to find out what her client Mr. Thomas needed, she took certain benefits away, hoping he wouldn't notice. No doubt this gave him the impression that his business wasn't important to her. Did Barbara assume she had no competitors and could do whatever she wanted to? And, Cindy did not tap into her sales fundamentals and previous experience that has worked for her business when presenting to a new account. Instead, she was counting her money before delivering her services. Who do you think Barbara and Cindy's biggest competitor is now? It turns out to be themselves.

A wise saleswoman would have considered the needs of her client, kept in touch, and provided personal and friendly service. She would have learned about his concerns with her department and worked to resolve them. And he would still be her grateful customer.

Bottom line, your competitive type determines the kind of saleswoman you are. Which type are you: aggressive, submissive, or wise? (Not sure? Ask others what they think of your sales abilities. They'll tell you your type!)

Most important, does your competitive type help you—or prevent you—from closing sales with men?

Know your competitive type well; it shows others if you are professional when servicing your customers and lets you pin point areas in which you might need to improve. Preferably, it will tell you that you're on the right track!

2. **Make decisions more quickly.**

Most men make impulsive business buying decisions. Why? Because men view shopping as a buying necessity while women shop for the experience. Even grocery-shopping behavior differs between genders. Men bring a list written on a scrap piece of paper or at least carry a mental list in their heads. They walk into a grocery store as if they are on a mission; they head straight for a certain aisle to pick out what they need and quickly toss items into their hand-carried basket. (I'm convinced those baskets are just for men.) Then they look at the next item needed and go directly to that aisle. They may traverse three or four aisles before they're ready to go to the checkout counter. They don't touch anything until they are ready to put it in their basket. Watch them and you will notice their shopping behavior.

"A low-cut dress blocks your brilliance. Dress brilliantly and people will treat you brilliantly."

~ Simon T. Bailey, speaker, author, *Release Your Brilliance*, Windermere, Florida

Recently, I was watching a man shop at my local grocery store. He was standing next to a produce clerk, pointing at the cantaloupe. Right away this intrigued me because most men don't like fruit. He asked the produce clerk,

"How long have the cantaloupe been stocked in the store?" The clerk quickly replied, "The cantaloupe is fresh from yesterday's delivery." This response apparently satisfied the man, as he grabbed a cantaloupe and put it in his basket. He didn't even weigh it to determine its price; he just wanted to know if the cantaloupe was fresh. This one observation showed me that men buy for value, not price.

On the other hand, women walk up and down the aisles, read the label on the back of a milk carton or soup can, and spend considerable time comparing brands. In addition, they take their time stacking items in their grocery carts, leaving plenty of room for more items. Women enjoy knowing what's offered; they'll circle the store until they've covered every aisle. While standing at the checkout counter, then they'll scan the magazine rack and talk to the clerk about the weather.

Karyn, a meeting planner in the hospitality industry, who works remotely from her home, knows how frustrating it can be to shop with her husband. Karyn said, "I won't go grocery shopping with my husband because he will run in and out of the store faster than I can get through the first aisle. He makes quick decisions, while I just enjoy getting out of the house to shop."

In general, women tend not to make quick decisions. They want to do research on the Internet, talk to their girlfriends for affirmation on what they are about to purchase, and ponder for days by doing a comparison check about their pending purchase. The reason is because women are more emotional than men about their purchases.

These examples show why you need to approach differently while selling to men. Men make decisions in a direct, quick, and factual manner. They want results immediately, so use this approach or they'll lose interest buying from you. For your own sanity, don't have them wait while you "wander" from aisle to aisle. The best advice, genders need to shop separately when possible.

In a man's mind, he makes decisions quickly because he wants to be known as being right and decisive. His superior attitude indicates he knows the answers to life's questions. Saleswomen who adapt to this important quality hold an important key to earning a man's business which results in huge profits.

3. Adapt your communication style.

People communicate from the day they're born until their last breath, yet, they still give mixed signals all their lives—confusion, miscommunication, misunderstandings. Yes, you may have read all the books, attended all the seminars, and paid top dollar for therapy, to the point you believe you've become a communication expert. However, clear communication challenges never stop, especially when selling to men.

Briefly, men want short discussions while women want to tell stories. If a man asks, "May I have your phone number?" a woman might reply, "I would be happy to give you my phone number, but I'll have to give you my new one, because my last phone number didn't work well, so my phone number has changed. This just happened recently, so my new number isn't in the phone book yet. You should be able to reach me easily with this new one, though.?" All he wanted was her phone number!

These tendencies were confirmed in a conversation between Tiffany and her husband, Jason. Jason wanted to add a brief note with his mom's birthday card and said to his wife, "Just sign this, Tiffany, but I don't want an essay."

Watch out for mixed communication signals. A few years ago, Robert Taylor went on his first snow ski trip ever with friends. He did not have ski equipment but figured he would buy a new set at the local ski shop. As he was walking into the ski shop, a beautiful saleswoman, Robin, greeted him with a friendly smile. Robin started to ask him about his ski abilities, but he did not want to embarrass himself since he would be classified as a beginner type of skier. So, he did not tell her everything she really needed to know to fit him with the right skis.

Robert, trying to impress Robin, bought new advanced skis and felt pretty good about his choice. However, when he skied down his first slope, he ended up sitting on the snow packed mountain more than skiing down the runways having a good time. Robert was embarrassed as his friends laughed at him, and ended up back at the ski shop eager to return the skis. Thank goodness Robin understood since it happens to her quite often. As Robin said, "Men sometimes miscommunicate purposely just to come across as a macho man."

Communicating with misunderstandings can be frustrating. Janet, a flight attendant, asked a passenger on her flight if he wanted something to drink during the flight from San Jose to Dallas. When Joe answered, "Yes, I would like a coke," Janet handed him a cup of ice and full can of coke. Joe thought how generous she was by giving him the entire can. Then Janet said to him, "That will be $2." Immediately surprised, Joe said, "You're charging me? Beverages have always been free on airline flights, and now you're charging me?" Janet responded, "The way the economy is right now, we would think passengers would already know how difficult it has been on airlines too." In this situation, it looks like the airlines need to train their employees to present any or new communication upfront. As a result, Joe refuses to fly that particular airline.

To adapt your communication style to the other gender's, you need to learn how he communicates. In March 2007, an article in the business section of the *Arizona Republic* newspaper described a small company, Cenpatico Behavioral Health, which employs 55 people yet reeled in astonishing revenue of $91 million last year. Terry Stevens, the CEO, learned early in her career the importance of how to communicate with men. Ten years ago, a male supervisor made his preferences clear: he wanted structure. And Terry took note of this communication style. Since the health care industry tends to be a male-dominated field, Terry said she limits emotional expression and sticks to bullet points and documents filled with facts, data, and outcomes, which most male executives she deals with prefer.

Terry said, "You certainly have to know the man's culture. Knowing how to 'talk' to men, like crafting an e-mail, which men tend to prefer over face to face communication, is appreciated. You put the most important point at the top, be brief, and use bullet points or they won't read it." Terry added, "When you're talking with men about a process in this format, you gain their respect. They accept you as one of their own."

Terry also offered this incisive advice for women: "Never be afraid to try something new. You can't say, 'I don't think they'll listen, they won't accept me, or it's more of a guy thing.' You must keep up with the times and the business you're in, and then being a woman won't make any difference."

Being able to communicate effectively leads to increased sales. In this new century of communication that involves technology, men love to talk about technology. As Terry mentioned, in the buying process, men don't need to be face to face to be convinced. You can use electronic formats like e-mails. However, it's not wise to do away with face-to-face communication, because it's an important component of the sales process.

When meeting clients in person, keep in mind that your body language and facial expressions are aspects of communication to consider as well as speech and writing. Men notice immediately when something is bothering a woman. He may ask, "What's wrong?" and she usually responds "Nothing." Yet men often know women are lying when they say "nothing," so don't go there.

Also, articulate your sentences clearly and don't rush when talking. If you're nervous, take a few moments to breathe. Be sure to address men according to how they'd like to be addressed. For example, if you're approaching a man in an older generation, you'd call him "Mister" while people in their 30s and younger are more comfortable using just their first names.

Be aware that men sometimes use "secret codes" in their conversations. They take the form of one-liners from movies or songs that illustrate points in the conversation. Sometimes they're so esoteric, you may not know what they're talking about. For example, a man may cite this line from the movie *The Godfather*: "Keep your friends close, but keep your enemies closer," or perhaps, "Go ahead, make my day" from Clint Eastwood's *Dirty Harry* movie. Even though men might totally connect with you it may not be wise to shoot a one-liner over their bow.

Christina Tzavellas, with CTZ & Associates, said this about these male codes: "Selling to men is a double-edged sword. Give them the information they need but use as few words or one-liners as possible. First, make your main point, then fill in with the minimum points needed to support your message. If he needs more information, he'll ask."

If you adapt your communication style just a bit, men will relate to you better. You'll become easier to work with and men will buy from you. Here are a few simple ideas:

- **Try spending *less* time building the relationship and *more* time helping him find exactly what he is looking for—answers.** Building the relationship is important; just spend a little less time in that area of communication. Men don't want you to know all about them at once, so give them their space until they feel more comfortable with you.

- **Silence is golden.** Spend at least 10 seconds within a conversation saying nothing. You may find this quite difficult. If you must talk, concentrate on a topic that will elicit a positive response from your customer.

- **Present a straight face.** Have you noticed how men tend to give you a straight face when talking with them? That's not a lack of interest in what you're saying; it's their way of not showing too much interest or excitement in case they don't want to buy your product or service. By mirroring their facial expression, you show you can handle their demeanor.

- **Stand like a man.** The way a man stands tells you if he's interested in your product and/or services. It's important to respect this and mirror his body language to a degree when standing and talking with him. Men are more comfortable standing in a "V" stance at an angle to you. Psychologically, they'll feel less pressured if you mirror such an open stance instead of a closed face-to-face pose. Men want a quick "out" if they choose to exit the conversation, so they leave themselves an "opening." So practice using an open pose, standing at an angle when talking to a man. Your goal is to have him so engaged in the conversation that he eventually stands face to face with you. But, most likely, he will want to protect himself with an open stance.

- **Complement your words with pictures.** Because men tend to use fewer words than women, along with your verbal explanations, communicate by using visuals, such as PowerPoint or printed photos, objects that move (as in video games), or numbers (such as in the game of poker). Men tend to pick up on anything that has to do with counting, which could represent money, too. Colors that appeal to men are green (which represents money), black, blue, white, silver, and even pink, which is a new men's clothing color. Surprisingly, red seems to not be as popular with men. Well, unless you are the best golfer in the world—Tiger Woods, who thrives on wearing red. So use their favored colors whenever possible—in your PowerPoint slides, logos, letterheads, or anything they will see connected to your company, products, or services.

Great communication takes courage and discipline. The key is to be upfront and use anything that will enhance your relationship so you can move toward closing the sale.

4. Stick to the facts; control the emotions.

Men are not interested in how a purchase will fit into their lifestyle the way women are. Nor do men have an emotional investment in their business purchases like women tend to do. Men are fact driven, so it's best to stick with the facts and control the emotions when selling to them. As explained earlier, men don't get caught up in the details of how facts were developed. Just present the facts in terms of what's in it for them. If they clearly see the value (and you have facts to back it up), you have a better chance to close a sale.

Anna Campbell with Women Business Owners said, "When selling to men, I need to have done my homework about who I am selling to, what interests them, and how they would benefit from my product and/or service. I also need to understand their economic situation, if they would be good strategic partners, and if this sale would be in their best interest. This tactic works for me in asking for the business."

Men want to know why they should purchase a particular product or service and how that item can benefit them. So do your research and give them recent facts, data, history, examples, or anything that supports why they should do business with you. Present their competitors' reports, too. This impressive tactic shows that you've done your homework.

Overall, put your emotions aside when dealing with men. It's too much pressure for men to handle an emotional saleswoman and they won't trust you if they are put in a position to feel sorry for you. Focus on facts, not emotions, to be persuasive. As Laura Scheller with Solmonte Hospitality, Inc. said, "Women tend to not be as direct as men. What works for me is keeping it simple—no long-winded sales presentations, stay factual, and get to the point. Men are usually in a rush and do not want all the fluff."

5. Use the written word.

Want to be completely convincing? Want to be in control of a sales situation? Want to win at the negotiation table? Then put your statements, thoughts, and viewpoints in writing. With so much information bombarding us these days, even your customers will have trouble remembering what was discussed in the conversation and presentation. Follow up by providing typed "notes" of your information is powerful and important, plus people generally tend to believe what they see in writing.

"A professional appearance and demeanor, along with respect for your customer, always works best. Wearing anything low cut, mini or short is, in my opinion, insulting to me as a professional."

~ Eddie T.L. Tadlock, Manager, Convention Center, Grand Rapids, Michigan

For example, Sue, an experienced sales trainer from Florida, had contracted with a hotel sales manager to conduct a sales training session. Soon after the contract was signed, the sales manager was no longer employed at the hotel. Sue contacted the hotel and was told that her services were not needed after all. Sue advised the hotel person to review her written contract. And, sure enough, everything was in writing and both parties were able to fulfill their obligations. If the details were not in writing, the employee training session would not have happened. You never know when someone will be leaving their jobs or if you no longer are able to assist your customers. That's why it's always important to deliver your promises in a written form, too.

An old, yet popular TV "reality" show, Candid Camera, set up situations to create humorous outcomes. For one stunt, they posted a sign on a road in the state of Delaware that read "Delaware Closed." People would come to a screeching halt in their cars and exclaim, "How long is it going to be closed?! My wife and kids are in there!" See how people tend to believe what they see in writing?

Holiday Inn Hotels Worldwide had a challenge getting their guests to acknowledge the checkout time of noon until its management discovered the power of the printed word. The hotel posted little signs in the rooms that stated, "Checkout is 12 noon." Now Holiday Inn has a 97 percent on-time checkout rate. People pay attention when they see something in writing.

When selling to men, treat your conversations to be important enough to write them down. Ask for a pause in the conversation while you write down an important point on paper. The fact that you're taking notes shows you care about what your customer says. In addition realize that at any point in the negotiation, your client is more persuaded by what he sees in writing. If a price change is coming into effect, for example, don't just tell him about it. Show him in writing. "Look at this letter I just received from my boss. Our prices are increasing, so let's confirm our contract today to save you some money." Whenever you can—show, don't just tell. People don't seem to ask questions once they see something in writing.

Documenting your conversations will help both parties. Share the document with your client as a follow up. This process is effective when you're giving him a choice as well. Seeing the options in writing helps him remember details, compare choices, and make decisions quicker.

6. Ask direct questions.

All customers have certain buying needs—either emotional or logical. Men tend to have logical needs when making a purchase. A man will ask himself, "Will this meet my needs and solve my problem?" So be direct by asking *him* questions that help you both arrive at the answer.

Beware of getting one-dimensional answers when you ask questions, especially when the conversation takes place electronically like text messaging. Electronic communication or not, men use fewer words in conversation than women. Their responses are short and to the point. As mentioned In Chapter 6, the key is to ask open-ended How and Why questions to help elicit more information than asking When/Where/Who and If questions. If appropriate, you can ask these good open-ended questions: "How do you see our company helping you become successful with your internal customers?" or "Why do you feel our products are important to you?" These types of questions will bring in information to help you service your male customers better.

However, a question can be *too* open-ended. Be careful about asking men, "What are you thinking?" If you do ask it, aim your question at the product/service only.

Asking men the right questions will appease their self-reliant minds, too. Being individualistic, men like to give their opinions. So give them plenty of time to answer your questions with no sales pressure and they'll usually reveal the information you need.

7. Engage in activities.

Most men feel less pressure in the buying process if they are engaged in an activity such as golf, poker, or even walking rather than face to face conversations across an office desk. When sitting in a chair, watch how they often move around or get up and *do* something to help them think about what is being said.

As mentioned earlier, during a sales process, don't put yourself in an intimidating position such as sitting across from the desk. Men prefer to meet in public places to get away from the office anyway, so take advantage of this preference. For important discussions such as negotiating a contract, invite your client to coffee, breakfast, or lunch. Be mindful of the time allowed and the location; you don't want to meet somewhere that's noisy or distracting, which may hinder closing the sale.

To build the relationship, play golf or attend a sporting event. Again, be prepared to know something about their interests like a sporting event or game. Don't ask a lot of questions and keep discussions brief during a event. Men are focused on the action. Because people love to do business with people who show interest in what they like, your goal is to concentrate on what interests your prospective buyer.

8. Focus on answers.

In general, for most women, discussing a problem presents an opportunity to explore, deepen, or strengthen a relationship. They're usually more concerned with *how* a problem is solved than strictly having it solved. This can make women either closer or less connected to the others involved.

However, men approach problem solving differently than women. It gives them an opportunity to demonstrate their competence and strength as well as their commitment to a relationship or situation. Men do not look for solutions as much as they want answers. Men have a tendency to dominate and want authority in a problem-answer process. It's not important *how* the problem is solved but *that* it's solved—and solved effectively with answers.

Men are able to separate themselves from the relationships related to the problem. Instead, they view the problem and the relationship with you as a saleswoman more independently than you might view it as a woman. This isn't wrong; men just don't always realize the advantages of partnering with a saleswoman— advantages that can be crucial to successful answers.

Sure, saleswomen want to make the sale but because they are nurturing and caring already, they want to please others, too. Also, if saleswomen know they'll be able to nurture the relationship into a good one while having the opportunity to sell a high-ticket item, they'll have more confidence to work harder solving their customers' problems with real answers.

9. Know about ambitions and goals.

When making a purchase, most men consider if the product or service will help them further their ambitions. They look at a purchase first from a practical perspective and then from a status/ego perspective, or ultimately how it will make them look good. Most men do have some idea of their ambitions or goals. If you ask men directly, you may be surprised at how they'll just blurt out their answers as if they'd been keeping it a secret from you until you asked. By sharing, they are trusting that you'll understand how important these goals are to them. In this situation, show your support—for most men, they enjoy being inspired by hearing a woman's encouragement.

As a saleswoman, get to the bottom of what makes your male customer successful. How can you make him stand out in his company or organization, with his friends and family, and, above all, with respect to his own ego. To find out what's most important to him, ask him.

10. Give recognition.

Although men won't always admit it, they do want recognition. This desire may go way back to the era when men were gatherers, hunters, and protectors of those most important to them. In fact, men will do whatever it takes to please their source of nurturing so they can be recognized. For example, in a personal relationship, they melt when their significant others give them genuine words of praise. In business, there is a saying, "flattering will get you everywhere." Know what your goal is and use flattering so you get what you want and more.

Men seek validation of their superiority or good performance. So in your role as saleswoman, remember to make him a hero. Treat him as if he is Batman, Superman, or Tarzan. Ask him if he had a choice, which character would he like to be. I guarantee he will pick one that best describes him. Also be supportive when a man is going through a rough time or a bad day at work. Respond positively to his successes. Being a cheerleader for him builds his self-esteem and shows you understand what he's going through. It paves the way for him to open up for a long and lasting business relationship with you.

When you recognize the good man that he is, he will feel energized to make a decision—to buy *your* product or service. Allow him to make the decisions when it's time to close the sale. Ask, him, "What do you want to do for our next step?" instead of telling him, "Here is what I will do for you." Acknowledge his excellent buying decision and he will think he has "won."

Chapter Eight

Protect Your Heart, Zip it Up to be Successful & Sexy

You are already successful and sexy in your own special way. That's right! In fact, you are more successful and sexy than you *can ever imagine.*

However, if you are like most women, you persist in viewing success and sex appeal as complicated. Women can go overboard *pretending* success and/or *dressing sexy,* just for attention.

It doesn't have to be that way if you apply all the strategies from the previous chapters. Just like women, in general, success comes in many ways, shapes, and sizes, depending on how you want to be successful. Try different ways to become more successful. Be creative and expand your business abilities, especially when selling to men.

Rachel, an advertising account executive at a rock music radio station, did just that with one of her customers. Her sales target is the male decision makers from 18 to 34 years of age. Included in that group was a prospective new client managing a major beer distribution center.

Young and pretty with a charming personality, Rachel showed up for her appointment with the potential client, fully anticipating he'd greet her with a smile. As usual with her appointments, she was prepared for him to look her up and down, always wondering (she surmised) *what if I could have her.* She knows that for the first 60 seconds, the last thing on a potential male customer's mind is business, but she's experienced the same greeting many times. Her looks open doors; she still has to accomplish the close.

Whew! she thought, *now that the first 60 seconds have gone by, we can talk about the purpose of the appointment.* She started the meeting with a needs analysis, asking what his goals were, what was missing in his marketing plan, and what competitive challenges he faced. She referenced past marketing campaigns and promotions to find out how they've worked for him—or not. She discussed the competitive landscape and his market share.

Then, after a lengthy conversation, Rachel's potential client indicated a "it was great to see you" smile, yet didn't see a place for her radio station services in his marketing mix. Rachel is intelligent enough to recognize that this was a courtesy appointment without intent to buy. But Rachel had a different idea. She had learned about his challenges, found an open window, and she was already formulating a plan for him.

When she returned to the office, Rachel began building her program. She accessed the research to show that her station reaches his target market—that, in fact, her station *over-*performs in the areas he's looking. She drilled down to the facts and figures that would support her creative promotional ideas. Then, with persistence and enthusiasm, she asked for another opportunity to meet with him.

First, she presented her creative ideas, knowing he would be excited by the concepts (the best thing salespeople can do for clients is thinking up answers for them). He nodded in agreement and she sensed buy-in was happening. She illustrated the radio market and unveiled the strength of her station. She had broken down the numbers to the most prime consumer of his product and had prepared a suggested marketing campaign, which she had laid out for the entire year. He was impressed by her ability to ask, listen, learn, capture, recap, create, propose, and implement. Imagine that!

Rachel left feeling confident. She planned to follow up in seven days, but before the week ended, she received this letter from him:

> *Dear Rachel,*
>
> *I have to tell you that I have not had a meeting with anyone quite like ours. I have not had anyone be so interested in my business and actually care to do the work to earn our business. You showed me the research that I was not even aware of in my own business. I did not realize that your radio station was so strong in the demographics we desire most, and your cross promotional ideas fit perfectly with the goals we are trying to achieve.*
>
> *I don't normally write letters like this, but I was compelled to put it in writing to you.*
>
> *We have decided to go with your plan, you can write up the order, and you have our commitment for the next year.*
>
> *Thank you again for your interest in our business.*
>
> *Sincerely,*
>
> *John*

At that moment, Rachel "got it" that men want to be sold, not sexed. She advised, "Ladies, we are blessed to be beautiful in our own way and need only to attach our beauty to our brains! Even though your entrée costs you 60 seconds of male distraction, protect your heart, zip it up by focusing on your knowledge, do your homework, be persistent and get down to business."

To effectively compete in today's world—a man's world—you have to identify and apply your skills, talents, character, and attitude—along with many more traits. Improving performance in any area, requires taking risks. To be the best, you must be *committed* to being the best—and that means you must *want* to be successful. There are many areas in which you can be successful, from being financially set to having a great job, being happily married with children, healthy and/or spiritually in tune.

"You get one chance to make a first impression; make it a professional one."

~ J.D. Freeman, President/ Market Manager, Clear Channel Radio, Dallas, Texas

However, just like your car, how fast you move depends on which gear you're in. Are you in first gear, second gear, drive, or neutral? Successful people do not stay in neutral—they're always moving forward to accomplish what they set out to do. Even if you start out in first gear, you're making some kind of progress. Therefore, take yourself out of neutral, shift your gears, and start moving to make a difference for yourself and your business. If you are moving forward—that's performance!

Becoming successful is actually easier than most people make it out to be. Yes, you have to show up, and yes, you have to deliver what you promised and follow up with your customers. But the key is how seriously you accept accountability as a saleswoman. Believe in yourself and expect other people to believe in you. Take on the challenging situations you encounter every day; they will make you a better salesperson if you accept responsibility for the best possible outcome for you *and* your customer.

Desire and belief create your success. The question is, "How successful do you want to be?" People respond to your stated beliefs and level of expectation. They feel it when you walk through the door, hear it in your voice when you pick up the phone, see it written all over your face. People respond to your positive energy.

But what's the ultimate cause? As a saleswoman, to become successful, you need to PAY ATTENTION! People pay little attention to each other and to what others say because they don't *believe* in what others have to say. If they did, they would pay more attention. Lack of paying attention causes problems, like having accidents happen on the freeway. And lack of paying attention prevents people (especially women) from being successful.

Pay attention and be observant throughout the sales process. To focus your own energies and move forward, know what's going on in and around you, and out in the world. Paying attention is considered a fundamental step to closing sales.

How many of these 12 "pay attention" business principles do you follow faithfully?

12 "Pay Attention" Business Principles to Help You Be Successful

1. **Have FUN!** Having fun will make you happy. If you're happy, your customers will likely "catch" your

happiness. Isn't that what life is (or should be!) all about? FUN! So, it needs to be first on your list.

2. **Create options for yourself.** Know your options for everything. Prepare for alternative ways of doing things or solving issues. Stay one step ahead and you'll be fine.

3. **Keep learning.** Knowledge conquers all! Age has nothing to do with it. Keep learning no matter what your age or gender, or what challenges you face with learning.

4. **Hang around "spiders.** "Spiders" are people who seem to know everyone and create a web of relationships. Don't only hang out with highly successful people, but gravitate to the "spiders." Walk around with them and say hello to others. It's an easy, fun way to meet different people, and you never know when a connection will pay off with new business.

5. **Follow up.** When you come in contact, whether e-mail, face to face, or other means of communication available with your potential customers or clients, immediately follow up with some kind of written documentation. A thank you note including what was discussed is a great way to keep you in contact. They will appreciate it along with knowing you were listening (paying attention) to them and their needs.

6. **Be a leader and a follower.** Determine what kind of follower manager style, you have because that will have a bearing on what kind of leader you are or will become. You can gain all kinds of skills as a manager that would be incorporated into your leadership traits. In other words, learn management fundamentals well; this experience will be a reflection on your leadership style.

7. **Keep yourself grounded.** Balance displays confidence, so always stand with both feet on the ground. Never lean on one leg or foot. Be careful about the shoes you wear, as they affect your balance throughout the day. Especially, avoid wearing high spiked heels that may present a health problem. Not only with your attire, but your sales fundamental skill as well. Review your basic sales skills from time to time. The basics will always be used in every sales process.

8. **Listen actively.** The two genders tend to listen differently, so it's worth understanding the differences if you're serious about growing your sales. For example, your male customers listen for the important points or information that will affect them or their company. They ignore all the small talk because it doesn't interest them. This behavior means they are listening "actively" for what is important to them. Likewise, *you* need to listen actively in your conversations with male customers so you know what to do in your next sales step with them. Listening actively helps by repeating points back to them to make sure you understand what they want.

9. **Be on time and end on time.** Ask how much time your customer or client has for your meeting or presentation. Make sure you stay within his timeframe. Immediately, this will help prove you deliver what you promise. In your meeting or presentation, cover the important items first while he's freshly ready to listen. If you wait, you might get interrupted, which is counterproductive to your goals.

10. **Invest in your spare time.** Saleswomen invest time in their kids, their homes, their businesses, and others,

but what about themselves? As a busy saleswoman, take time just for yourself. Zone out once in a while by finding time for yourself. Relax and enjoy being alone. Even for only 10 minutes a day, take time to reflect on your lifestyle, goals, family, friends, and anything else that's important to you. Men do it while sitting on the couch with the remote control in hand, right? You will be amazed how this time will reenergize you. Never allow someone else to be your priority when it's *your time* to be still, quiet, and alone with your thoughts.

11. **Do what's wise instead of what's easy**. Wisdom is about making good choices, and they are not always easy. But if you are wise and work hard, you will feel the accomplishment. Be confident, resilient, and learn from your mistakes. How else will you know who you are internally? Value yourself, mistakes and all. If you do this, nothing will stop you from being successful.

12. **Be in good spirits.** Your attitude will demonstrate who you are as a person and a saleswoman. Use positive self-talk to motivate yourself on a regular basis. Be your own number one fan!

In a sales presentation, men notice if the saleswoman is paying attention or more importantly, ignoring their buying signals and continues to sell even if they are not ready to buy. If this happens, challenges and issues arise. Therefore, the main issue "is u"—which means the issue you're having was created by you. You have a choice; you can create your own issues or create your own success.

Problems equal pain plus solutions equals profits. So pay attention to problems, as they are most likely painful.

Providing solutions for your clients alleviates their pain and results in profits for you. Don't wait for your customers to help you in solving their problems. It's up to you to pay attention, recognize problems, and then find the answers.

> *"I believe in life lessons! Many times a women believes she can grab your attention in a low-cut dress. All I do is grab to protect my wallet."*
>
> ~ Roger Rickard, SVP Sales, don anderson incorporated, Sacramento, California

Just as you find the answers for your customers, you can find answers for yourself. Pay attention by training your mind just like you do your body when you exercise. Also, pay attention to everyone around you—friends, neighbors, and co-workers.

I recommend following these seven personal principles to further enhance your success.

7 "Pay Attention" Personal Principles to Becoming Even More Successful

1. **Believe in your spirit.** Have a belief in the spirit within you, and God will strengthen it. Take the time to discover it, use it, and share it with others. Your spirit is one of love, wisdom, peace, gratitude, and joy among other sparkling attributes. Your belief in and sharing of your spirit will enhance and expand your life immensely.

2. **Dream.** Use your spirit to dream, and believe in your dreams. How do they sound, feel, taste, and smell? Allow your dreams, or goals, to come alive by sharing them with others you know will be supportive. Write them in your journal so you can view your dreams and goals every day. Don't deny that what you've written can happen; just say it, believe it, and then do it.

3. **Create a plan.** Move your spirit and dreams into a plan. What actions will you take; what's your projected timeframe for completing them? Your life is a journey that unfolds. Unfortunately, where people think the destination—the results—are most important no matter how one gets there. But it's more enjoyable to focus on the journey itself. And as you create a strategy for achieving them, *also* be open to inspiration and guidance. Know that if you focus on the journey going forward, your plan will unfold as it should and the best results will come.

4. **Focus on your talents.** As you move through life's journey, continue to refine and sharpen your skills to reach your dreams. Both your dreams and your talents, which came from your spirit, are meant to be realized. As a saleswoman, what talents and skills can you put to use in the business world? Be aware of your strengths and your knowledge. How can you use them to the fullest? Capitalize on your natural abilities and interests, and build your skills around them.

5. **Be disciplined.** Are you willing to put forth your talents and efforts with a strategy to pursue dreams given to you by spirit? If you answer, "Yes," then you're ready to train yourself to be disciplined. With self-discipline, you won't stray off the path and scatter your energies. You'll have the courage and will to win. And one day, you'll find yourself living your dream.

6. **Visualize success.** Visualizing yourself living your dream encourages your spirit to rise, your dream to come alive, and surprising results to unfold. Don't neglect to apply this to your advantage. Take time to

practice it. Just focus your imagination on your life's dreams and create them any way you want. You have the power to bring your desires alive!

7. Reward yourself. It doesn't matter if your goal is to lose weight, cut back on expenses, or achieve a big sale; it's important to celebrate every level of success throughout the process. The greater the achievement, the bigger the reward you deserve!

While one of my coaching students, Danette Mitchell, was learning these 7 "pay attention" principles, she shared with me her spiritual beliefs and told me about growing up as a disturbed child. As an adult, she has continued to strengthen her spiritual belief which has taken her many years to do because of the dysfunction in her family. However, she spoke of someday becoming her own boss and a proficient writer and published book author.

So we built a strategy for Danette to reach her goals. I gave her homework. Danette displayed a discipline that revealed her talent on paper. In one of her assignments, she wrote several wonderful stories that allowed her to express herself in a healing way. She developed a vision because of these stories (and others) trapped inside her.

Within one year, Danette brought her vision to life; she's in the process of becoming a published book author. She's also building a network marketing business that's part of her self-development strategy. Danette explained the rewards this way: "I discovered myself and how to help others. I didn't know I had the courage and inner strength to share such personal and bizarre details about my life. Yet I did it. I read a quote that said, 'What would happen if one woman told the truth about her life? The world would split open.' For me, the world *has* split open. Reaching my goals and, in doing so, helping others see that they, too, can fulfill their dreams is greater than being judged or rejected."

Applying a positive attitude, building expectations, and paying attention, you feed all the right areas of your soul that make you grow—that make you successful and "sexy." Even in the sales arena, the male consumer will respond to your services and love your products more than ever. Clinton Kelly, fashion expert from the popular "What Not to Wear" television show, said it this way: "When you are put together, it looks like you're not trying too hard, and that's what's sexy."

So don't do the old worn-out strategy of wearing your sex on your sleeve. Instead, protect your heart, zip it up. Protect yourself by doing the right thing—for you! Embrace how you may become more successful and as sexy as ever. Know who you are today and what you want to become tomorrow.

BONUS!
Advice for the Low-Cut Dress Woman

Chapter Nine

Advice from a Myriad of Men and Aunt Dee

From the book title, you may have thought this book was about how to dress for success. Not exactly. Now, you know it's more about what *not* to wear—and why. You know it has a lot to do with self-respect and professionalism. And you know what *does* make a woman successful— especially in sales. This chapter provides a refreshing way to help the low-cut dress woman further understand the impact of what she wears in a business situation.

Women are judged on the way they present themselves, usually more notable than the way men dress. Fans of NBC's *Today Show* may remember when Meredith Vieira first appeared on national television wearing white shoes in late September 2007. This may not seem like a bad thing, except she wore these white shoes *after* Labor Day. Fashion protocol dictates a woman can't wear white shoes after this particular date. Viewers took immediate notice of this broken fashion "rule"; phone lines lit up and e-mails poured in with comments regarding her choice. In fact, the viewers made such a big deal of this fashion faux pas that the *Today Show* did a story about wearing white after Labor Day for the next day's broadcast.

Look at the Hollywood celebrity magazines that give so much attention to "who wore what and when" among the rich and famous. It's amazing how similar gossip and stories about men rarely surface. However, there are women who bring judgment upon themselves by wearing incorrect apparel at inappropriate times.

Continually changing styles create the latest fashions because, when styles change, people buy new clothing to stay in vogue. Despite this merry-go-round of change, one style remains constantly popular: the low-cut dress—along with the intention behind its design. Women love to don low-cut dresses for evenings out on the town to impress their dates and friends.

Despite its popularity, many prominent women have been highly successful without having to tap into the "low-cut dress" strategy. To name a few: the late Princess Diana of England; the queen of talk shows Oprah Winfrey; Governor Sarah Palin; Senator Hillary Clinton; novelist and educator Maya Angelou. This is not to say they never wore low-cut dresses; they just didn't use them as a business success strategy. Princess Diana was remembered most for her contributions and her innovative fashion statements, wearing stunning clothing to fit each occasion. By day, she dressed professionally in tailored business suits. By night, she attended parties or the opera in her own style of the low-cut dress—a sleek, colorful, classy gown. Actually, she was one of the first women to wear stylish lingerie, which started a trend for many women who didn't have the confidence to wear it. This strategy did not interfere with Princess Di's mission to claim leadership for her country.

The same was true for the late first lady Jacqueline Kennedy Onassis when she was the wife of President John F. Kennedy.

She too wore clothing to fit the occasion in any situation. Today, both these women are still considered icons and classy due to their strong stance looking proper. For all of these admirable women, their class gave them respect around the world. They become stellar role models for women in the business world who draw attention to who they are as professionals. They also know when and where to wear a low-cut dress.

———

Men naturally respond to the low-cut dress because it stimulates them. They won't deny enjoying women who dress well, showing off their attractive body shapes. However, it's unfortunate that men will notice and talk about the dress instead of focusing on what the woman has to offer the company or his business. But then, can you blame them? Despite men's appreciation of a woman's body, in the business world, most men believe the low-cut dress hurts a woman's credibility. They question her knowledge of the buying process and even the product itself. They wonder things like this: Why does she use this tactic? Can I take her seriously? Is there something wrong with her entire organization?

Now You Know

Saleswomen, you no longer can say "I didn't know." I suggest following these tips and opinions that came directly from the men who think you need to hear them.

- You limit yourself if you depend on your looks.

- To advance, use your head, not your chest.

- Beauty fades; dumb lasts forever.
- How you dress is how you will be treated.
- It all comes down to what you know, not what you wear.
- Be the whole package, and the "right" dress is part of that.
- Being a walking billboard for fashion designers only lets others know you are less than creative and more of a copycat.
- Beauty is not a trait of leadership; knowledge and hard work are.
- If your ship is sinking, no one cares how you look or dress. People only want to know what to do next.
- Leave your expensive jewelry at home unless you want everyone to know you have low self-esteem.
- Don't wear baggy or tight clothing if you feel overweight. Both baggy and tight clothing add to the perception of extra weight.
- Panty lines showing are never sexy.
- Too much makeup, join the circus.
- Wear only clothing that is clean.
- Too many patterns in your wardrobe make you look like a Disney character.
- Groomed hair and nails, and clean shoes are a must!
- Be aware of wearing sleeveless tops, high heels, and revealing necklines. You will be the talk of the conversation—and not in a good way.

Now, don't get men wrong; women should enjoy wearing a low-cut dress. However, wear it when and where it's appropriate, which is not in the business world. If you ignore this advice, as this list tells you, men won't take you seriously in anything you say or do.

Remember, what you wear in any situation helps determine your experience and your results. How you perceive yourself also plays a part. If your results are not to your liking, it's up to you to make the right changes.

Consider what happened to Becky Cain, a lawyer in Florida. Becky said, "I used to be a size 6 and experimented by wearing 'Tina Turner-type' clothes at work (low-cut blouses, short skirts, very high heels). I received lots of attention from many men, including my boss, my co-workers, and even my customers. I got everything I wanted and advanced my job status. Now that I'm a size 14 and wear my conservative business suits again, it hasn't been easy." Everyone's "loyalty" had been based on the wrong thing, and it was no one's fault but Becky's. From the beginning, had she emphasized her knowledge instead of her body, her foundation at work wouldn't have crumbled when her body changed.

Flaunting your sexual attributes is one thing, but you needn't restrain yourself from being feminine. You deserve to be who you are without having to wear clothing that displays your attributes like a billboard. Don't sell your self-esteem down the river by getting all washed up. You definitely deserve better than that. Protect your heart, zip it up.

A woman's business attire should, in part, be determined by the industry she represents, and should always be combined with confidence and knowledge. If a man thinks a woman should dress in sexy clothes, he's not worth working with, no matter what the job.

Meet My Aunt Dee

Besides my wonderful mother, the woman I most admire is my Aunt Dee. Way ahead of her time, she understood this matter of business attire and women's self-esteem.

In the early 1980s, when few women were creating business opportunities in the marketplace, my Aunt Dee did. Long ago, she had learned what to do when selling to men in any situation. A confident, strong-willed, intelligent woman, she could have outclassed any swimsuit model, but her professional image was first and foremost in her mind.

> *"There is an extremely long list of situations where the low-cut dress is appropriate. At the bottom of that list is making a sale."*
>
> ~ Ross Shafer, Comedian, Ross Shafer Productions, Anaheim Hills, California

With her knowledge and professionalism, she broke through the glass ceiling and became the vice president of four divisions of a home building company in Dallas, Texas. For nine years, she oversaw the work of hundreds of employees while managing three companies within each sales division. A strong negotiator and excellent leader, she brought people into teams to close every sale and improve the bottom line. These abilities hugely affected the employee bonus structure of her company; the bonuses benefited every employee at year end.

During her initial hiring interview with the company, her future (and younger) boss asked, "Where do you see yourself in this company five years from now?" Without hesitation, she replied, "I want your job. Do you not think a woman can do what you do?" He sat back in his chair and looked at her with amazement. He replied, "You have a lot to learn before that can happen." Dee proceeded to say, "Then I would like you to teach me what I need to know." He immediately hired her because of her directness and honesty. He saw a woman who had the potential to be successful for the company and for herself. He and Dee began a long, wonderful working relationship in which both held full respect for each other.

Aunt Dee

Throughout her years employed at the company, Dee worked with a variety of younger men. One time, an office rumor started that Dee was sleeping with the boss. Little did the rumor mill know, the boss's wife and children and Dee's family had attended church services together for years. But true to her professionalism, Dee never acknowledged the rumor because she knew that the rumor mongers would have to recognize her contribution to the bottom line and her hard work for the good of all in the company.

A year later, the arrogant young sales manager who had started the rumor came into her office and apologized to her. He said his wife had told him he was wrong; he'd come there to admit it. From that hurtful experience, Dee's goal was to protect other women from going through the same thing. Her message to her staff was this: "Know that you were hired because you are smart and capable. Always be willing to do anything you may ask someone else to do and then do your job, and do it well. You will be acknowledged for your capabilities. There is no better way to climb the corporate ladder." Dee was eventually promoted to regional vice president of administration over all the company divisions in Texas and in Atlanta, Georgia.

It wasn't long before she had to share her message again with a young, beautiful woman whom she had hired as an assistant to herself and the president of the company. Dee had plans to promote Mary in the next couple of years if she worked out.

In the meantime, Dee was put in charge of a project outside of the office, involving several hundred young employees. She instructed those participating in the project to wear long black pants and white, short-sleeved shirts, even though it would be hot that day in Texas. Mary, who was well endowed, showed up wearing a sexy halter top and shorts.

Now, Dee knew Mary was having an affair with her boss, the president of the company. She obviously believed she could dress to please him that day and get away with it. But Mary neglected to think about how the way she dressed reflected on Dee's reputation—and that of her department.

So the day after the event, Dee called Mary into her office to make known her disappointment in Mary's deliberate dismissal of the dress rules. "There is no way anyone can hear your voice when they're looking at your body! You have no authority dressed like that in a business environment. Further, you are a reflection of my department when assigned to one of my projects." Mary brushed off Dee's admonition and accused her of being jealous. Dee didn't even acknowledge Mary's accusation.

When Mary's tearful outburst was over, Dee said she had hopes for Mary and plans to promote her, but first Mary needed to learn how to be a professional. Dee warned her that she had to stop trying to sleep her way to the top, and that she didn't need to wear anything low cut or short to become successful. She told Mary to go home and think about whether she wanted to continue to work with her. "Make a decision by tomorrow," she said and closed by saying, "By the way, that would mean obeying company dress rules." Then Dee looked her in the eye and said, "No more low-cut dresses or halters at work or at any company functions while I am the boss."

> *"On the flight deck, a woman's uniform covers the body, but her skill always shows through."*
>
> ~ Jeff Brelsford, Er, Captain, FedEx Express, Hong Kong, China

Later that day, Dee approached the president of the company and confronted him about his unacceptable behavior in the corporate environment. She took a risk and told him he'd have to make a choice between Mary and her. Dee knew she could be out the door that day. But, she also knew her boss respected her professionalism, her management skills, and the impact her hard work had made on the company's bottom line. So he promised to stop the affair and not interfere with decisions she made in their department about Mary.

When Mary returned to work the next day, she agreed to obey the dress rules and expressed her desire to continue working with Dee. Goals were set up for Mary to strive for, and a year later, Dee promoted her to a management position.

Two years later, Mary came into Dee's office, sat down in front of her desk, and thanked Dee for what she had taught her about how to reach for her goals in the company. That brought a huge smile to Dee's face. She loved helping other women become successful, too.

———◦———

In another situation, Camille, a young new manager had joined the corporate team. Camille attended several meetings with Dee and got to know the managers and how their departments functioned within the division. While sitting in an executive operations meeting, Camille noted how much appreciation the men had for Dee's input during the meeting. She was impressed with the courteous responses from all the men when Dee was present.

Because Dee was on equal footing with the team of managers, it became evident to Camille that Dee's department and her input were vital to the company's operation. But something bigger was operating—respect!

The following week, Dee had not yet entered the room for the weekly operations meeting, and Camille became painfully aware that she was not receiving the same respect that Dee commanded. After the meeting, Camille came into Dee's office and asked her, "Why do these men use foul language with me, but when you enter the room, they cease immediately?" Dee observed that Camille was trying to communicate as the men did—to be one of them. She said Camille didn't understand that she was a smart, capable woman and not one man in that room could do her job as well as she did. She didn't have to behave or speak like a man to be a vital part of the operations team.

As you can see, Dee became known for her ability to work with and develop women to help them move up in corporate environments. She gladly shared her tips, which have made her successful in and out of the board room, while working with men and women of all ages. Dee's success tips are provided in the chapter that follows.

Chapter Ten

Tips for the Low-Cut Dress Woman

"You don't do any favors for yourself when you do wrong for yourself."

~ Dee Taylor, Professional Speaker,
Author, Coach, and Consultant, Dallas, Texas

Dee Taylor is a highly successful business woman. She's also my wonderful Aunt Dee, whom I'm so proud of. She has achieved prominence in many areas of the corporate world as an executive, television and radio personality, and nationwide recruiter. She has gained insights on subjects from how to get an interview to how to supervise hundreds of employees. All of her experiences have enhanced her abilities to understand how to promote to and sell to others.

Today, she owns her own business as a professional speaker, author, coach, and consultant from Dallas, Texas, sharing her expertise with nonprofits and small businesses. She has served on boards for the senior community and enjoys her heart's passion—speaking to and about family caregivers.

I believe Aunt Dee is a role model for women of every color, race, age, or creed. She gladly provides advice about what worked for her in all her diverse business adventures. Woman can soar to greater heights because of her shared expertise.

TIP #1: Don't allow anyone to try to make you be like them.

And don't try to mimic someone else for the sake of being accepted. It is so important to be who you are at all times. (People show up back in your life sooner than later. Remember that!) Even if you have to stand alone in some situations, love yourself enough to be able to say, "I am okay in this situation." Know that nothing is forever and this too will pass. But it never, ever pays to try to be someone you are not; e.g., to wear a low-cut dress and high, high heels to an office function, which makes both you and others totally uncomfortable. This is not displaying confidence, and it certainly doesn't demonstrate you can handle a responsible position. You will be noticed alright, if that is the way you want to be remembered.

Bonus Winning Tip: Remember, your natural beauty and abilities to produce the desired results are enough at any given time. But you must believe in them first!

TIP #2: Do not participate when you don't need to participate.

You may stand alone, but you will be respected, even though you may feel separate from the pack. It's been said that it's better to be a listener than a talker; you learn more that way. Sometimes it is better to be an on-looker to get the total perspective of what is actually going on in a given situation. If you don't want to participate, then don't. You'll be respected for that and, believe it or not, you'll stand out above the rest. Never be afraid to take a stand on your own views.

Bonus Confidence-Building Tip: Always state your position when asked and don't be afraid to look the individual in the eye when you do it.

TIP #3: Treat everyone with respect.

When encountering a difficult circumstance, always give the other person the benefit of the doubt and listen to his or her side. The Golden Rule always applies: "Do unto others as you would have them do unto you." This indicates respect for their feelings and you will learn how they view the business situation, which may or may not be like your own view. Put on your listener's hat for these circumstances and maintain eye contact, whether the person is male or female.

Bonus Business Tip: If you become a careful listener, it will help you respond in a professional manner and may even engender a team environment you did not expect. This is good while protecting your heart, yourself!

TIP #4: Display a constant, powerful position at all times.

People will know what you stand for when you value relationships. But don't ever give away your power. Stay confident in your position. Be responsible to the company, and lay ground rules accordingly with those under your authority. Caution: Don't set standards so high that no one could meet them, not even you!

Bonus Relationship Tip: You can work side by side with individuals without giving away your power. It's easier than you think—try it and see.

TIP #5: Develop fellowship with women in the office.

Watch for and seek out women who are supportive and

believe in you. Share resources so they see you as a woman-friendly professional who cares about their jobs. The following rule always applies when working with other women, whether they are under your authority or not: "Don't ever ask anyone to do anything that you wouldn't do yourself." Women will follow you if you lead with this attitude.

Choose women who truly want to and have the potential to be empowered in your company. Don't be afraid to mentor them and help them develop into managerial positions. After all, you can't plan on a promotion within a company if you haven't groomed a replacement for yourself. For example, if women need help with how to dress or act in office environments, take time to teach them. They will look up to you and help make you look better, too. Choose the right time to convey this, though, and always do it privately.

> *"Saleswomen need to take advantage of being who they are while applying new sales techniques from preparation, execution and closing instead of the other way around."*
>
> ~ Ian Gordon, Manager, Baesystems, LTD, Edinburgh, Scotland

Bonus Success Tip: Never lose sight of the fact that the buck stops at your desk. You are, after all, in charge of your work environment. Cheer for other women!

TIP #6: It's your responsibility, so make your own rules.

Keep office hours and happy hours separate. It has always been my practice in the corporate environment not to party with co-workers who are under my authority; and that includes during after-work happy hours. Yes, I attended company parties as required, but I stayed only as long as necessary to make an appearance. Another rule: Adhere to the same work hours that you expect from your employees when possible.

Bonus Leadership Tip: Remember, when the boss is away, the employees will play! How they handle this circumstance will be a reflection of your leadership capabilities.

TIP #7: Pay attention to those around you, and don't be afraid to be the professional you are.

Always pay attention to people around you, acknowledging everyone, even the most "insignificant" employee. You may need that person to help you with a project some day. When working with men in the corporate board room or office, maintain your personal standards so you will be respected at all times when you speak with authority in meetings. When I was a corporate executive, if anyone got out of line verbally, it took only one look from me and they would apologize.

Bonus Respect Tip: It is essential to never be disrespectful to your teammates, co-workers or boss.

TIP #8: Know that you don't have to be one of the "boys" to survive in the corporate board room.

Draw the line by dressing and conducting yourself professionally. Then the "boys" will not cross that line, I promise you.

Bonus Knowledge Tip: Be the woman leaders want on their teams because of the smarts you bring to the table, not what you wear at the table. Yes, they will notice the dress, but then how can they hear what you have to say?

TIP #9: Stop undervaluing yourself; put your knowledge first.

Without equal pay, you don't have equal status. Be mindful of this and don't accept less. Use your work experience, education, and know-how to push yourself up the chain of command. Remember, women like me made a huge impact by taking risks to brake the glass ceiling back in the 1980s, so you don't have to do it again. Just climb, baby, climb, whenever circumstances open the door for you, don't forget to help others when you get there. You are good and you know it. Let everyone else know it, too, through your daily performance on the job.

Bonus Expertise Tip: Impact that bottom line for the company and you will be noticed for a job well done. Both men and women will remember that more than how you dress!

TIP #10: Do what is wise instead of what is easy. Don't react right away in any given situation.

If a man puts you down, don't lash back at him immediately. In fact, you may have to walk away without saying a word. Leave him without the reaction he was expecting. Rise above it. Take time to evaluate and think through what is best for the good of all. This will reflect your ability to work with any gender any time.

Bonus Behavior Tip: Remember, you are only as good as the people who work for you. Your behavior and dress on the job show them what a professional looks like. So treat others with kind and wise consideration—even when they are rude—and you will get much more from them.

TIP #11: Have a purpose.

Always keep your goals in front of you and focus on them daily. Know where you want to go while on this planet. Identify what you want so you are focused instead of having to go through the backdoor in a low-cut dress. Let your performance, not your dress, dictate your next promotion, and then no one can denigrate your achievement. This simple aspiration will help keep you on the right track: Always take time to help others when they need it.

Bonus Performance Tip: Throughout life, don't let pride affect your performance. Just earn your achievements, and the accolades will come from others who admire your kindness, tenacity, and capabilities!

TIP #12: Be true to yourself.

You can only lie to yourself. Just like the low-cut dress, you know it's wrong, so why degrade yourself in front of others. Choose your decisions wisely. Stand tall and fight for yourself.

Bonus Pride Tip: Be proud of who you are. Love yourself!

In Summary

What's Really in Fashion?

So, there you have it— how to sell to men without having to wear a low-cut dress. Now you get to choose! Do you continue to apply the old "low-cut dress" strategy? Do you risk your reputation in any given situation? Or do you want to use your skills, your knowledge to win the business and the big bucks? Are you personally proud of your accomplishment?

How you want to be perceived is up to you. Go ahead and wear that low-cut dress—but only when it's appropriate.

It has been a great pleasure to introduce these new findings, personal stories, and information gleaned directly from hundreds of men and women interviewed for this book. The material presented is meant to inspire the two genders to work better together in conducting business so we all become Champions together. My passion is to provide encouragement for you as a saleswoman to validate your own beliefs and live your own values. If you want to be successful, take this information seriously. Try all the ideas one at a time, and apply them to the best of your abilities. Through embracing this new information, you can gain or regain your self-worth, and your dreams will come to life. Dig deeper into your own wisdom, express yourself, and be who you really are and aspire to be. Find real beauty in just that. Inspire yourself to be successful by protecting your heart, zip it up!

I constantly share with my audiences the importance of embracing the journey, as the results will come. Thank you for reading this book. I hope it spurs your journey to success and huge profits when selling to men.

Deborah's
Preferred Free Sales Resources

www.freesalesarticles.com

www.bazaarvoice.com

www.salesvault.com

www.npd.com

www.softwaresalesjobs.com

www.eyesonsales.com

www.justsale.com

www.salesresources.com

www.bestofsales.com

www.inc.com

Let's Hear Your Stories

Now, it's your turn to share your stories, experiences, or nightmares while selling to men. Help other women learn from your practical strategies that have worked for you.

More importantly, I would love to know your thoughts on this book—if you found it helpful and inspiring. With your feedback, I will continue the series of How to Sell to Men.

Please e-mail me through my web site at www.DeborahGardner.com or www.HowtoSelltoMen.com.

I look forward to seeing you in full fashion!

– Deborah

Speaking, Training and Consulting Opportunities

COMPETE BETTER NOW! LLC

is a leading sales training company that supports the better of business relationships. Deborah Gardner, CMP, better known as "The Competition Gal," is president, speaker, trainer, and consultant.

Deborah works with individuals and organizations worldwide to help thousands of people "win" through programs that translate into higher sales, stronger negotiations, exceptional customer service, teamwork performance including greater personal and professional development.

Deborah uses a variety of skill-building approaches to help you move to a higher "Champion" level. Whether it's a keynote presentation, active workshop, teleseminar, or a consulting project, she can TRANSLATE competition and TRANSFORM your team or event's performance!

Just some of Deborah's programs include:

- COMPETE BETTER NOW ... for the BEST Performance of Your Life!

- Sales + Techniques = Results

- Networking to Bond!

- Re-Discover your Visionary Talents to Master your Business

- How to Compete in a Man's World

- Salesology: Is There Light At The End Of The Sales Tunnel?

- The Greener Side of Life

- The C-R-U-S-H Factor

- How to Become the Choice Your Customers Simply Can't Live Without

- Naked Negotiation: The Bare Bone Truth & Essentials for Effective Negotiating in Business and in Life

- Putting "Green" into your Routine

As a certified meeting professional (CMP), Deborah understands what a successful program requires. Her experience, triple "A" guarantee, energy, and commitment explain why hundreds of companies and organizations hire her. As an educator, motivator, and champion for identifying untapped potential, Deborah will help you rediscover your essence for winning and competitiveness.

Contact Deborah directly at Deborah@DeborahGardner.com or call 623-869-9141.

Printed in the United States
134239LV00003B/1-162/P

9 780982 144008